Woodcock Shooting

Woodcock Shooting

Steve Smith

Stackpole Books

Library of Congress Cataloging-in-Publication Data

Smith, Steve, 1947–
    Woodcock shooting / Steve Smith.
        p.   cm.
    ISBN 0-8117-1907-3
    1. Woodcock shooting.   I. Title.
SK325.W7S55   1988
799.2′ 4833 – dc19   88-6061
                                                                     CIP

*For Chris and Jason,
a couple of pretty good woodcock hunters
who have made the miles shorter*

Contents

Foreword

My mind's eye always captures Steve Smith in a short-brimmed hat, thigh-length Barbour jacket, and Wellies (knee-high rubber boots that British sportsmen are born in) that surround the legs of his double-pleated trousers. Surely a well-attired sporting gentleman like this carries a custom-built side by side of European origin. Nope! Smitty carries a sixteen-bore Parker that sports a lump of something (wood or possibly walnut-hued putty) on the comb. Why? Because it works. A character, a rogue, or possibly an eccentric? There is no doubt all of the above apply to my gunning buddy and treasured friend, Steve Smith.

Smitty *should* write a book on woodcock and how to hunt woodcock. There can be no man alive who thinks, dreams, eats, and sleeps longbills with the passion Smitty does. He even wrote his master's thesis on the movement of migrating woodcock. Since that time, he has not only continued his philosophical and sporting pursuits of the woodcock, but he has also moved into the sporting literary world in a very commanding manner.

Smith came to national prominence as the editor of *Gun Dog* magazine. At about the same time he began authoring heartwarming books on outdoor subjects. It is impossible to cite a contemporary author who is as well-informed of his subject, who is as able to spell out a yarn with such pleasant, down-home humor. Now Steve has launched a new career with *Shooting Sportsman* magazine. Only Steve Smith could gather together the Who's Who of shotgunning lore and showcase them all in a superb new classic magazine.

Educator, writer, editor, magazine founder—that alone does not qualify a sportsman to write an entire book on the Prince of October. The thousands of hours of pursuing, studying, hunting, and reflecting on woodcock are the gifts Steve brings to this book.

I know Smitty loves woodcock because whenever we're hunting upland birds, he always compares the bird at hand as less sporting than the woodcock of his native Michigan. In his younger days, Steve was always spouting off shooting percentages; those percentages are evidently less important now because he doesn't keep track anymore. No one moves more woodcock for time spent than Smitty. He not only understands where the birds are, but he also takes more 'cock with fewer shells than anyone alive. Well, at least he did up until a couple of years ago. About that time he was joined by his two teenaged sons. I think the responsibility of molding and guiding Chris and Jason has probably distracted somewhat from percentages. Now when Steve talks about hunting the woodlands of Michigan, his eyes squint and his mouth uplifts into a huge smile around the ever-present pipe as he tells of Jason's or Chris's latest escapades in the coverts he shares with his sons.

You ought to read this book because Steve Smith loves the yellowing foliage of late September, the point of about any old breed of true woodcock dog, and any shotgun as long as it has two barrels in the same place as your eyes. You ought to read this book because of the knowledge Steve has gained in thirty years of hunting these birds, and—most important—because of the woodcock themselves. You ought to buy this book and treasure it because my true friend Steve Smith is a gentleman who loves the outdoors, who knows, understands, and lives for woodcock. Finally, you should save this book and pass it on to your sons and daughters in the same way Smitty is passing on the world of the woodcock to his sons.

Dr. Jim Nelson
Elm Creek, Nebraska

Woodcock Remembered

We were walking across an open woodland in Michigan. It was late October, but the rain and the fog made it seem like November. We were crossing from one cornfield to another, our game bags nearly full of rooster pheasants. I was a boy, and these were the Glory Years.

To my left, my father with his Model 12 almost stepped on a woodcock, the first I had ever seen. The bird rose quickly, at the speed of light compared with the wet roosters we'd been shooting at all morning. The big twelve waited and then boomed, and the little form plummeted, wings tucked against his sides, like a tiny, incoming missile. My dad picked up the bird and called me over: "Steve, come here. Have you ever seen a woodcock?" I ran over, looked, and was converted. For life . . .

. . . Mark Sutton's little hound was baying a rabbit. We were in our early teens, and even though it was early in the fall, we were

running bunnies because that's one of the main things we did in those days. I was standing atop a stump, waiting for Dixie to bring the rabbit back around, when I decided this was the wrong stump. Hopping down to do something about it before the rabbit got there, I dashed across a stand of willows in a low spot where a little water had collected. A woodcock flushed, and I went to work with my twelve-gauge autoloader—the perfect gun to me in those days. The third and final shot dropped the bird, my first. I went on over the next two weeks to miss twenty-three birds in a row—three shots each—before I got my next one . . .

. . . My setter was working a patch of alders that bordered a forest trail. On the other side of the alders was an open glade of bracken ferns, still standing under light frost, for it was mid-September. I led my son, Chris, around the alders and posted him on the edge of the glade. The dog's bell had now fallen silent in the alders, so I walked in to flush. The bird came out low and fast, over my shoulder and streaking toward the glade. The boy swung his twenty double ahead of the bird as it made for a tiny maple tree at the far edge of the opening. The twenty cracked just as the bird cut behind the branches of the tree, but the load of light nines penetrated the bright leaves, and the bird reappeared on the other side, wings clapped to its sides and curving down like a tiny, incoming missile. Chris's first . . .

. . . Jake, my younger son, had missed something like twelve straight shots at woodcock during this, his first season. Chris, now fifteen, and I had worked hard to get him shots. The birds were plentiful, but he was always in the wrong spot. Finally, on a clear October afternoon after school, we found ourselves along an alder run. Chris and I worked the cover deep; Jake worked the edge where I had put him, figuring any of his shots would be straightaways, his best chance of taking a bird.

He almost stepped on a male bird that was hugging the edge, and Jake dumped his first barrel two feet over the low-away woodcock. But I watched as he cheeked the stock of his twenty double a little deeper, gritted his teeth, and touched off the left barrel. The bird clapped his wings and dropped . . . a tiny, incoming missile. Jake raced for the bird and held it high, his eyes welling with tears. But it was hard for Chris and me to see . . . our eyes were misty, too.

Hunting woodcock is hunting memories. Those of us who hold the bird above all others have our own memories, some strange, some nothing more than a bright sun and flawless colors. Woodcock days are easy to remember. If you'll freshen your drink and come along with me, I'd like to share some of mine with you.

1

The Finest Bird

In England, where they do a lot of driven shooting, taking a double on woodcock is regarded as something of an achievement. The birds are different, larger than our own, and they are driven from cover sometimes in the course of a pheasant shoot. Then and only then are the beaters allowed to speak, and the clear cry of "'cock up" alerts the guns. If you take a pair with a right and left, you are entitled to boast a bit and have others buy you whiskey.

In this country a double on woodcock is tough to get. I have yet to get one. I have shot staggered singles several times, the second bird flushing when the shot at the first bird startles it, but this is not a true double. I suspect that many of those who claim doubles on woodcock are misinterpreting what a double really is: both birds in the air before any shots are fired. That's just one of the many things that make woodcock different from other birds.

A woodcock has a strange set of adaptations that nature has physically distilled through the forces of evolution. These physical and behavioral characteristics make him a mystery to most of us: unpredictable at best, a chimera at worst.

The woodcock is most like the shorebirds, but he has left the stretches of barren, moist lake shores for the uplands. Yet he still prefers the wet places to feed, for the wet areas draw the worms that are his main food, and these places are never far from where you'll find him.

His bill is prehensile, the tip constructed to act independently of the base so he can probe deeply into the ground for worms and—even with the base snug against the ground— still open the tip to latch onto a meal. To help him locate this meal a little better, his ears are in front of his eyes, up by his bill; his ears help his bill to hear food.

The woodcock's eyes are high set and large. He is a crepuscular creature, one who prefers dusk and dawn, the moments between daylight and nighttime. Words like "dusking" are soft words, used to tell of the woodcock's evening flight to food. When you hunt him on cloudy days, the bird is likely to be especially peppy, able to better navigate through his brushy cover once you've flushed him; on bright days he is more likely to twitter up at half speed. On such days of bright sun and glorious colors and half-speed woodcock, memories that last forever can be built, and talk of a limit of birds for as many shots passes between hunters who know the score.

His large eyes connect to a brain that is built upside down, his cerebellum squeezed and oozed to the top of his head, where it has had room to grow. This part of the brain controls his motor muscles—his wings—and his flight is deceptively adept. There is no crashing through twigs like a grouse; the woodcock twitters his way around them. That twitter, one of the few sounds that can drive me to distraction, is caused by the wind sucking through primary feathers and not by the bird's vocal cords.

His legs look somewhat like those of a wading bird, his feet large enough to hold him up on wet soils. The feet of a newborn woodcock are so large that an adult band can be

A woodcock hen on her nest in open-forest leaf litter. Typically, the hen will lay four eggs, which are oddities in themselves, being quite large for the size of the parent bird. The eggs are split by the chick from pole to pole rather than along the equator, as with other birds. The survival rate of young woodcock is among the best of any of the gamebirds. And, as shown in this picture, the hen's camouflage is among the most perfect in the bird world. (Photo, courtesy of Michigan DNR)

used during research. Even the young are something to behold. Like all ground-nesting birds, the young of woodcock are precocial, able to move about freely as soon as their down dries. Unlike other birds, the woodcock chick splits his egg from pole to pole instead of along the equator, more or less a function of that large bill being tucked away in that tight egg, an egg that looks way too large for the little hen to have laid. The hen normally lays four eggs, which hatch into chicks that are among the most likely to survive of all gamebirds, and the ratio of young birds to adults each year is a marvel.

Riddles

The woodcock is a bird whose migration from the North to the South is little understood. Biologically speaking, this migration is relatively new: The lands from which it originated are still rebounding from the weight of glaciers that covered them not too many centuries ago. But geologists think in terms of eons and zoologists in epochs. The woodcock hunter wants to know how to find birds.

There is no color variation between males and females. The females are larger because they carry developing eggs to the north, courtship and copulation having been taken care of miles to the south on some singing ground. And the mother, being the only active parent, broods the large egg and protects the large chicks with her body. Logic dictates that the female be larger than the male, and the woodcock is, above all else, a logical creature. Each of his adaptations is for a reason. He is not put together from spare parts, nor is he the flighty character the name "timberdoodle" implies. Such names are given by those who seek him and wonder about him and care about him only in autumn, when he can be shot and cleaned and eaten. Those of us who wonder about him all year love him more.

Speaking of eaten, the woodcock is often served barely broiled and with the entrails intact—that's right, friend, the insides. This portion is called the "trail," and on toast it is supposed to be the best delight to the palate in the uplands. I'll pass.

And there are those who look at you as if you poisoned them when you give them woodcock. They have a hard time with the taste. This reaction is fine with me, for there are fewer hunters and eaters of woodcock as a result. I have some recipes that make woodcock taste like veal and I use these on friends who are a little squeamish. But I like woodcock as they are. I can buy veal anytime.

Woodcock have the large heart and the dark breast of the bird that migrates, but the legs and thighs are white meat, an indication of a bird that walks little. The breast meat and the thigh meat are so different you can't believe they came from the same bird. Another enigma.

But the explanation is again most logical. The woodcock migrates by flight and goes to and from feeding coverts by flight. Once he is where he is to feed or rest for the day, his movements are short and restricted. He flies much and walks little, and his body parts tell us this.

His coloration is perhaps the most perfect of all birds. A woodcock grassed on a forest floor leaf-littered with the hues of October is nigh invisible. Many is the time when an air-washed bird has left too little scent for my dog, but I have seen the bird come down. I will walk there and start looking, but I rarely find the bird this way. So I start scuffing the leaves with my boots, and eventually, I will kick the bird or I will stir up enough latent scent for my dog, and I will pocket my prize. There are times when I have sworn a dead woodcock has plummeted through a tear in the time–space continuum into another dimension. But no, he is only in the brown leaves, invisible.

This coloration protects him and makes the hens brave on their nests. It makes the bird confident enough that he will hold for a pointing dog, unlike the larger grouse and the gaudy pheasant. I always get the feeling that a woodcock never believes he's been found by a dog. Even after you flush him and shoot him, I think he believes the whole thing is one huge mistake.

Woodcock do strange things to the people who hunt them. The birds make us spend megadollars on guns with better family histories than our own and dogs with far better bloodlines. We buy station wagons or four-wheel-drives for getting to the coverts, and we spend great, towering stacks of money on woodcock prints and woodcock placemats and woodcock mounts and whiskey glasses with woodcock on them. These birds make us watch the nighttime skies and smell the evening breeze, trying to reawaken a sense of smell that has been dead for millennia. They make us swat bugs and open veins as we storm through hot, thick cover. Let's face it, if the Army made us do what we do to ourselves hunting woodcock, we'd probably write to our congressmen.

Woodcock make us put up with white dog hair on all the dark things we own for eleven months a year because that dog is needed for the four Saturdays of October when we hunt woodcock, and you could send the dog to Yale for what we spend on vet bills, food, training aids, gadgets, and furniture he chewed up.

But most of all, woodcock are mystery, and maybe there are mysteries that ought not to be understood. The mystery of the bird's autumn migration, the flights, is the greatest of all. I've spent most of my adult life in one way or another, formally and informally, watching these birds and charting their flights.

Skydancing

Woodcock head north from their wintering grounds in the South as the increasing length of sunlight triggers hormones that stimulate the reproductive organs of both males and females. Many times the birds shuffle back and forth, north and south, as late-winter and early-spring snowstorms greet them. From the Carolinas and Louisiana and Georgia they come, solitary migrators, heading north like so many winged salmon, looking for the very coverts where they were spawned. It is not that exact, but the birds are headed for familiar ground.

Along the way there is the spring courtship ritual. The male birds perform their mysterious skydance for the pleasure of the coy females. When I watch this at dusk in the spring and I catch a glimpse of the male approaching the female, I always have to chuckle at this little guy courting his oversized spouse. Perhaps knowing he would lead a henpecked life, he leaves her after copulation.

The skydance starts off with the male bird announcing his presence with a short insectlike buzz that is impossible to describe, sort of a nasal beeping sound. While he is doing this, he is strutting around his little domain, a small, clear area known as a singing ground. In areas where clearcuts are made for wildlife, these singing grounds are often where the wood chipper was placed and the vegetation killed and flattened by the big machines.

Many males, probably subdominant young birds, do not sing at all but hang around watching, much like a spike elk watches a royal herd bull, looking for his chance.

Singing grounds are most often near a young forest. Less than two city blocks from my home, there is a field that was a pasture when I was growing up for a local farmer's sweet-breathed old Holsteins. He gave up farming, sold off the land, and moved away to where his kids could do their homework by electric lights, and the cows no longer grazed.

Eventually, the pasture started to go back to the wild, and the annual grasses were succeeded by small shrubs and then young aspen.

Here, in the spring, the woodcock sing on warm nights—the warmer the better. It isn't really a nesting area because I have yet to find a nest; instead, the birds seem to be passing through on their way north and have decided to put in a few nights of courtship to see if anything good comes of it. This old pasture has some hiking trails through it, and it is these that the birds use as their base of operations. Last spring three males sang for a week as late as mid-April; birds are recorded singing in my area as early as mid-March, and some will even sing during a snowfall.

I think that these males are young birds, and this is their

first spring of courtship. They haven't yet established areas of their own where they have had success, so they choose areas of opportunity as they migrate north in the spring. But I can't prove it, so I'm probably wrong.

Anyway, our buddy is next heard springing into the air, his wings sending to your ears that familiar autumn twitter of the flushed bird. He starts flying in a circle, large at first, then gradually tightening as he climbs up and up, revolving around his lift-off point. At the top of his spin he starts singing a sweet, melodious sound. Suddenly, he stops flying and singing and plunges toward earth. Arriving nearly where he began, he alternately buzzes and moans at the female, and she whimpers in return—you've got to be close to hear this part of it. If he is successful in convincing her he's just what she wants, good genes and all, they copulate and the female leaves for where she will build her nest and rear her young. If the pickings are good, the male—the blighter—will stay on, hoping to entice another young lovely.

When I was in school, I used to use Phyllis, my stuffed female woodcock, as an enticement for males. It was comical to watch the cock of the walk try to get that lady interested. More than one fellow wore himself out skydancing for her, the coldest fish in all of woodcockdom. The guys used to strut up to her, try to mount, and then walk away with that "sheesh" look on their faces and take off for another try, starting right from the top.

During this time of year adults can be caught for banding in very fine mesh nets (mist nets) placed in open areas through which the birds are likely to fly during the courtship. This is about the only really effective way to band adult male birds, but it does not yield nearly the number of banded birds each year that brood banding does. Still, it is a valuable tool.

The female, for her part, looks for a nesting site in the open, near brushy land. Grasses near the singing grounds are good spots, but the best locations are the edges between openings and forest. It takes a few days for the hen to pre-

During a bird-banding operation, the dog, staunch to the left, has located a hen and her brood. The biologist carefully searches every square inch of cover, lest he step on the young birds. Good dogs are a must for bird banding because it is the only way that the well-camouflaged brood can be found. (Photo, courtesy of Jerry Warrington)

A captured adult hen is banded. The band shown in the picture will identify this particular bird if the bird is recovered later by a hunter or is captured by another bander. The hen is so confident of her camouflage that it is often possible to capture the hen as well as the young during bird-banding operations. (Photo, courtesy of Jerry Warrington)

Biologist Tom Prawdzik of Clare, Michigan, and his banding partner, his setter, with a woodcock chick he has captured during banding operations. Prawdzik will band dozens of birds in the course of a spring. (Photo, courtesy of Jerry Warrington)

A close-up of the band on a woodcock chick. The chicks are aged by measuring their bills, a surprisingly accurate method. An adult band can be used even on a chick as young as this one because woodcock chicks have inordinately large feet when born. (Photo, courtesy of Jerry Warrington)

pare her nest, a depression in the forest duff. She likes over-head cover, which is often a good indicator of nesting areas.

The hen usually takes about five days to lay her four eggs, and then about twenty days to incubate them, culminating in the hatching of the eggs. There is a marvelous nesting success rate among woodcock, the best of any of the gamebirds. The young are born with a bill fourteen millimeters long. For the next fifteen days this bill will grow two millimeters a day. Banders who capture young birds can age them very accurately by simply measuring the bill, subtracting fourteen, and dividing the remaining number by two. This equals the age of the bird in days. For example, a bill length of thirty-four millimeters means the bird is ten days old ($34 \text{ mm} - 14 \text{ mm} = 20 \div 2 = 10$ days).

The young birds are soon foraging for food. They grow quickly, and within a month they are practically full grown. Short flights are possible for the young birds within a month of birth, and certainly by six weeks old, a young bird's flight and looks make it indistinguishable from an adult. In the fall I will often hear a hunter claim to have bagged a young bird because it was small. Not so—the bird was a male.

Woodcock chick mortality is quite low because woodcock usually choose good nest sites, they are well camouflaged, and their broods are small, making it easy for the hen to keep an eye on them. Additionally, their rapid development quickly puts them beyond the point where things often kill the young of other birds, like cold rains and marauding predators that eat flightless chicks.

The worst predator is the common housecat, a tabby from a nearby farm. Each year these animals kill uncounted hundreds of brooding hens and young birds. They are unnatural predators that exist in the artificial conditions humankind supports. I can tell you, a housecat that has gone wild and is stalking the coverts has as its greatest predator a woodcock hunter with a shotgun.

Habitats and Hangouts

During the summer, the woodcock normally spend their days in aspen, alder, or aspen–alder association. Feeding takes place before dawn and after dusk and at times throughout the night. Alder is a good feeding and resting area because the birds cannot tolerate high grasses down at their level. They must have open ground in which to walk around. After alder reaches maturity, it starts to decompose, putting acid in the soil that drives off worms, so mature alder is rarely used by woodcock, the younger stages being better cover as well. A moist field just returning with head-high alder is a fine summer and early-autumn cover—a fine cover anytime, for that matter.

If you had to dig yourself a can of worms to go fishing with, where would you look? Well, you'd probably try rich, loamy, moist soils, right? So does the woodcock. Pasturelands near second-growth hardwoods—alders, willows, and so forth—are the preferred feeding areas. River valleys provide the constant moistness the birds need for their food because woodcock are voracious eaters. There are reports that woodcock have been observed in captivity eating up to twice their own weight in worms and other invertebrates (grubs and the like) each day. Certainly six ounces of worms for a six-ounce bird is about right for each twenty-four-hour period.

Normally, the birds fly from a resting, daytime cover to the feeding coverts. I have seen woodcock probing in shallow puddles on dirt roads after dark.

The worms, then, draw the birds that have been lolling away the day in protective cover, waiting for nighttime. Once, while pheasant hunting in the middle of the day, I shot a woodcock out of an open cornfield and the bird still had a live night crawler in its bill, so all you hear about evening feeding is not always true.

Interestingly, fires and timbering, especially clearcutting, have a favorable impact not only on the vegetation that returns but also on the soil conditions. Nutrients so returned to

Some evidence that woodcock were here—tracks and probe holes in a low, muddy spot in the forest.

the soil tend to stimulate worm populations. The best wood-cock management is good timber management.

During the late summer there appears to be a shuffling as the broods break up and the young birds scatter somewhat to adjacent coverts. This dispersal probably helps to prevent inbreeding and also strengthens flight muscles in preparation for the migration to come. During this time woodcock are seen at evening with great regularity. All that awaits is the triggering mechanism that will tell the woodcock, "Be gone from here." Quite probably, the factor triggering fall migration is a threshold in the declining hours of sunlight. Even if weather is very cold early in the fall, the woodcock normally will not go until that threshold is reached, usually mid-October in the northern states and a little later farther south.

The flights are often affected by factors that can really mess things up. Two years ago there were floods in my area of the world, floods that inundated entire villages. Many of my best streamside coverts were underwater. I did my best woodcock shooting early in the season, as the flights came through early. With familiar land, the best available, underwater, the birds didn't tarry long.

Similarly, in dry years the birds go through fast. They learn there is little food available, so they head out quickly. In dry summers birds will often shuffle north, south, any direction, looking for the moisture that holds their food. Some birds even go to high elevations to take advantage of low-hanging fog and heavier dew that wets the ground.

One of the best ways to locate pockets of cover in dry years is to stand on a high point with good visibility as the sun comes up. Rising mist can show you where pockets of moisture and therefore likely feeding coverts are located. In dry years the birds seem to stay in the feeding cover longer, sometimes all day. They may be reluctant to leave one of the few good things they've got going.

In normal years, when the late summer has been adequately wet, the flights are more of a trickle-through, the shooting not spectacular but sustained over a more extended period of time. It is these years that woodcock hunters relish,

Another sure sign of woodcock: whitewash on an aspen leaf. Woodcock droppings are extremely susceptible to any type of moisture and are easily washed away, even by a heavy dew or frost. The smart hunter who encounters splashings such as these gets ready because they usually mean whatever made the splashings is nearby.

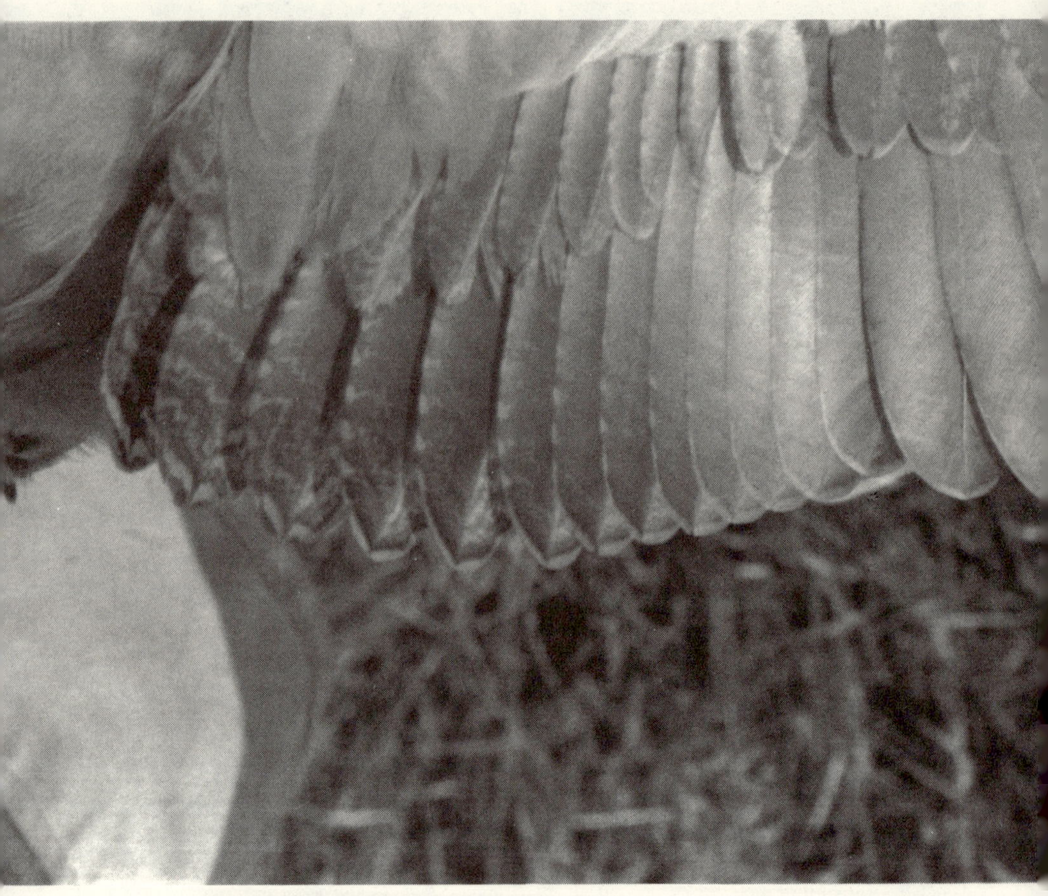

The flight feathers give the woodcock its whistling sound. The well-defined subterminal band at the tips of the secondary flight feathers mark this bird as an immature or juvenile bird.

for their sport is stretched out. In dry years or in years when a sudden freeze comes along, the flights are heavy but of short duration, and when the birds are gone, they are gone.

Anatomy of the 'Cock

Knowing the bird in hand is worthwhile. The females are larger overall, their bills are longer, and they appear chunkier in the air and when you hold them. The males are smaller by about 25 percent and are more streamlined. Males are also faster and tend to go out from your dog's point low and fast, as opposed to the females, which appear to tower more regularly. Of course, early in the flights the females are the more likely targets, and since the cover is still lush, towering could well be the way in which the bird takes the best available escape route.

Young birds—birds of the year—have the tips of their secondary flight feathers well defined in a subterminal band of buff; the adult birds have a more indistinct, mottled subterminal band in the same place.

Although what I have to say can help you be a better woodcock hunter, it should also make you a more appreciative woodcock hunter, one who knows a fine bird more intimately, not as a clever target and worthy adversary but as a friend. Trusting you in this way, I give you the story of how woodcock flights can be, to a great extent, predicted so you can be where they are when they come through in the autumn. The method takes work and, like all things in nature, it is not foolproof because the birds can always change the rules. But the times I have relied on this over the last fifteen years, it has helped me and those to whom I have shown it.

Ducks and geese possess great strength; doves have the aerodynamics of a reentry vehicle. The woodcock's physical adaptations for long flight measure up poorly with these other birds—but he makes up for it through behavioral adaptations.

An animal survives the cascading millennia by coping with its environment and what it has to dish out. If the

The wonderful prehensile bill of the woodcock. It has many sensors for detecting worms underground, and its tip is capable of being opened even if the base of the bill by the nostrils is wedged tight into the ground. The eyes, high set and to the rear of the skull, are perfect for looking in all directions while the bill is in the ground.

A female woodcock, left, dwarfs the male. Many shooters find that early in the season their bag is made up mostly of females, but later on males make up the majority of the birds shot.

animal's body doesn't protect and help it, it must adjust its habits accordingly or it loses the race for survival. Through evolution the survivors pass on the winning traits to their offspring, which sharpen these skills to the benefit of the species. There are individual losers, but nature cares only for the species. Woodcock, then, have developed a method of migrating that allows them to overcome their less-than-streamlined shape. Here's how it works.

Mapping the Wind

Woodcock essentially use the wind as an ally. During the autumn months across woodcock range, the shifting of the weather patterns means that more and more winds start to blow from a northerly quadrant—north, northwest, or northeast. Woodcock, as a general rule, do not migrate at a high elevation. In fact, telephone lines kill a number of these birds each year as they migrate in the evenings just after dark.

This height likely gives them the advantage of using navigational aids. River valleys that lie in a general north–south direction are often used as migrational guides as well as sources of food.

Once the autumn days shorten, some impetus—the decreasing daylight hours, the angle of the sun, or whatever—tells the woodcock to go. Then, using the friendly tailwinds of autumn, the birds embark on their flight south along friendly valleys.

But what of the layovers, the times when the woodcock flight is in? They may stay for several days before moving out again. Normally, these times are associated with winds that have swung around and are blowing from the south. Since these warm winds offer little danger of freeze-up, and since they represent headwinds to migrating birds, the woodcock stay put and wait it out.

At times, perhaps because the birds are far off a main north–south river valley, they are likely to use a feeder creek for navigation and feeding, using winds from a quadrant that will push them to the main north–south valley.

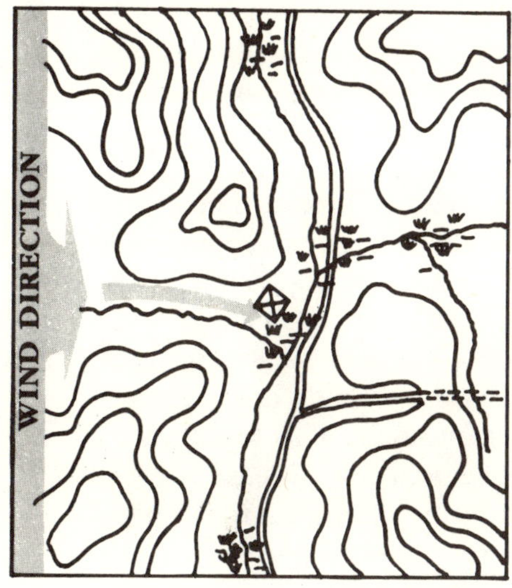
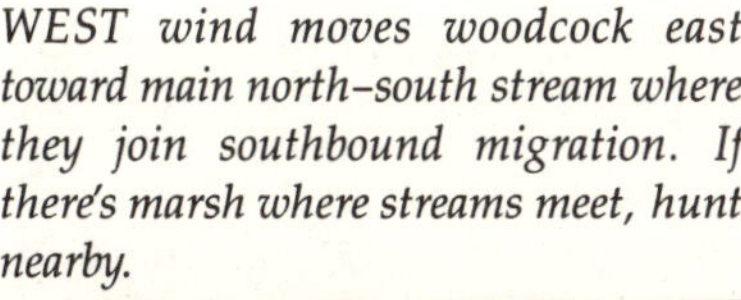

WEST *wind moves woodcock east toward main north–south stream where they join southbound migration. If there's marsh where streams meet, hunt nearby.*

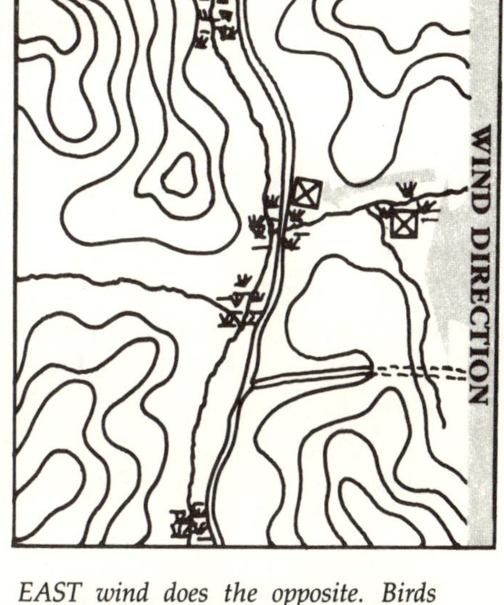

EAST *wind does the opposite. Birds move westward to join main north–south migration route. Use topo map to locate likely streams with marshy shorelines.*

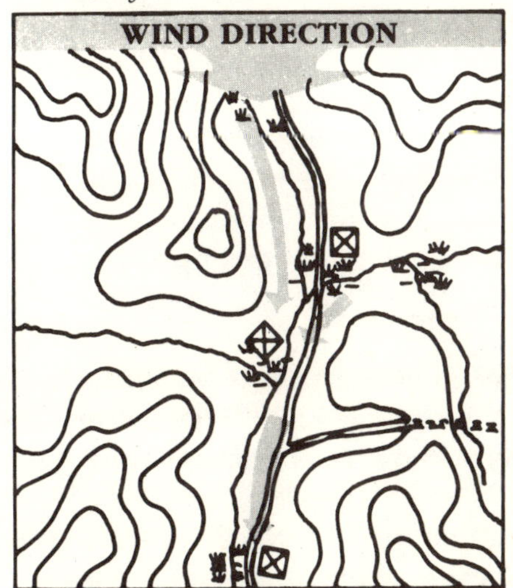

NORTH *wind gets birds moving all along main north–south stream. Make for marshy ground and hunt in the shelter cover near feeding grounds.*

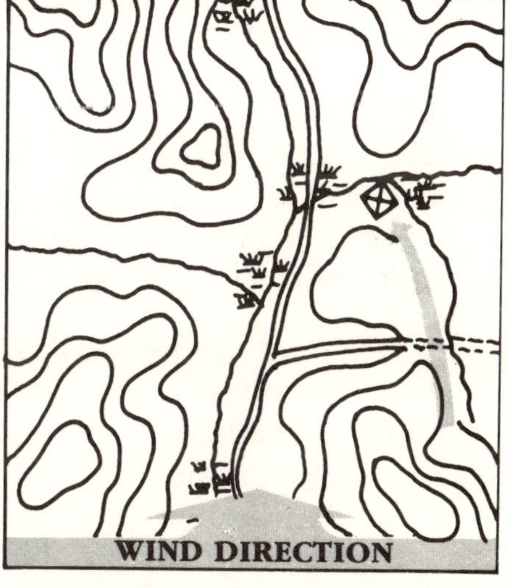

SOUTH *wind halts birds on main stream. If you already know where they are, hunt there, but best bet is north–south creek that later joins main stream.*

Using the accompanying maps as a guide, you can see, for example, that in instance number one, woodcock living along the feeder stream would wait for a westerly wind to take them to the main north–south valley, where they will wait for the northerly wind they need to propel them along the main valley. In example two, an east wind is needed to move the birds out of that feeder stream's valley to the north–south valley. In both cases the birds are most likely to be congregated at the spots marked X—excellent places to hunt.

Map number four shows that sometimes even a south wind is needed to get the birds moving. The birds take a south wind up to a feeder stream, wait for an east wind to take them to the main valley, and then wait for a north wind to take them away.

Tom Huggler, a friend and fellow woodcock devotee, has even found that woodcock use north–south highways for navigation and feeding. The ribbons of concrete are easy for the birds to follow at night, and the roadside ditches—with young vegetation that accompanies the cutting practices of some highway departments—are a perfect combination for woodcock.

The chunkier female woodcock migrate earlier in the year. Doing so not only protects the breeding stock, it also gives these birds longer to make the trip. The smaller, polygamous males are better able to fight any headwinds, so they are able to stay north longer, probably to better imprint in their brains the singing grounds they'll use next year for breeding.

Hunting woodcock, then, becomes a matter of watching the winds. If the wind is from the west at night, it's best to hunt the confluence of a westerly moving stream where it enters a north–south valley.

If the wind is from the east, hunt the place where a stream enters the north–south valley from the east. If the shooting is good one day and a south wind picks up at night, you'll probably be safe in returning to the same area the next day—but don't overshoot any one covert. Woodcock are solitary migrators; they don't travel in flocks like other birds, so if your coverts held no birds on Friday and then six woodcock on Saturday thanks to a friendly wind, it is because the cover looked good to six individual woodcock.

Additionally, all of these factors seem to work better when skies are clear. Perhaps the woodcock use the stars for celestial navigation, as do some other species of birds.

One aspect I'm studying right now is the odd instance when the birds fly and there are no apparent valleys for them to follow. Maybe there are residual traces of an old water-way—say, a large amount of soil moisture, which promotes the growth of the right cover—as well as a bunch of worms for food.

I know that one migrational route seems to take wood-cock near my home along what nine thousand years ago was the existing shoreline of Lake Huron. That shoreline is marked today by the occurrence of sand ridges, the remnants of long-lost beaches. It could be that the beaches act as navi-gational aids for the birds, and on most there is cover grow-ing, farmers having not bothered to clear and plant this almost-pure-sand soil. Interestingly, the influencing curve of the old shoreline, as I've located it through geological, aerial, and topographic maps, is generally north to south.

In any event, understanding woodcock and maybe even being able to guess when the birds will migrate to your co-verts does not at all detract from the sport and the mystery of woodcock hunting. Quite the opposite, it only adds to the affection and wonder we hold for this bird. Spare parts? Not very likely!

Waves of Woodcock

Sometimes the vagaries of wind and weather can cause the shooting to evaporate as quickly as it came. In the old parlance of a "fall" of woodcock (as in a "gaggle" of geese, an "exaltation" of larks), when the birds drop in unexpectedly, there can be dozens where before there were none, and when they trickle through, there will be a half-dozen where yesterday the coverts were empty.

But these vagaries not only bring birds to us, they also take them away from us, the winds and weather sweeping the coverts clean of birds. There have been many times when I had great shooting one day, and the next day, in the same places dotted with splashings, the birds were gone. Often a hard north wind will take birds away and bring others in, so there is no knowing that these are not the same birds.

More often the flights will take birds away and bring others in their place, but not for several days, so there is a lull in the shooting, even though the migration may be in full swing. You are simply between waves of woodcock moving ahead of the winds.

There is one covert that I hunt each fall a few times. It lies hard against a clear little branch of the Tobacco River, and from the gravel road, it does not at first look like a woodcock covert. Strictly speaking, it isn't, but it is a dandy flight covert, a place where I move birds only during the migrational period. There it is not uncommon to move twenty birds in an hour and do it several days in a row.

When the birds are in and I am having good shooting, I pray for south winds to stall the birds where they are; a north wind sends them on their way down the route carved by the stream, and I will be without birds—but usually only for a few days, until the next "fall" of 'cock shows up, pushed there by the same winds that picked them up from farther north and brought them to me.

If you have done your homework and have built your network of contacts, then you can keep an eye on the birds throughout their migration south. Far to the north there are people who can tell you when the birds have left their coverts, and you can figure—at twenty-five to fifty miles a night—when they will be arriving in your coverts. Game biologists or other hunters are, naturally, your best source of such information. They should be remembered at Christmas with Scotch whiskey.

Using topographic maps put out by the U.S. Geological Survey helps in finding both highways and natural rivers or valleys with flowages. The maps, available in the large, seven-and-a-half-minute-quadrangle configuration for all of the eastern United States, are great for locating woodcock coverts, marking them, and then following up on likely places. Almost every good woodcock hunter I know will use these when the situation calls for it.

A few years back I used one of the maps to find a hidden flowage between two hills stretching parallel to a river that was normally a good woodcock migration route. That fall a huge flood had inundated the normal areas I hunted, and the woodcock had shifted their routes. Even though I had hunted that river valley for years, I had no idea that the flowage—an intermittent stream, one that flows only part of the year—was there. The maps showed me how to find new coverts close by. In a normal year that flowage would have been too dry for the birds, but because of the heavy rains and flooding, it was just right, and the birds were there.

No covert should be hunted too hard. The smart woodcock hunter, one who loves the birds and wants his sport to last, has a string of such places and he hunts each sparingly. Woodcock migrate as individuals, and a place that looks good to one may well look good to several. The best woodcock cover is, from my experience, alder mixed with second-growth aspen, young trees up to fifteen feet tall. Woodcock need thick cover with high "stem densities" for protection. One biologist of my acquaintance told me that woodcock would hang out in a field full of fence posts if the posts were close enough together.

The alder–aspen stand offers the birds what they need in terms of protection, the alder normally indicating the moist soils that draw the worms that feed the birds. In Wisconsin there is one superb little clearcut of perhaps thirty acres. It is predominantly aspen, but there are clumps of alder mixed in. During the middle two weeks of October, you will find a woodcock or two under every clump of alder. I'm not going to tell you where it is.

Clearcutting

Second-growth forests like this used to be the result of fire or windstorm. Today, the socially acceptable alternative to nature is clearcutting, the process by which every tree in a given area is cut down. The Forest Service and various state wildlife agencies carry on clearcutting as a means of turning old, mature, sterile forests into game-producing young forests. Such forests are good for ruffed grouse, deer, rabbits, bears, songbirds—and woodcock.

Wherever the pulp paper industry is active, there you will find woodcock cover. In Michigan's Upper Peninsula, for example, the activities of several large paper companies have turned most of the western end into a huge woodcock covert. Find a clearcut from five to ten years old, and you'll find woodcock. They are in pockets and have to be hunted, but they are there.

Normally, when an area is clearcut, the woodcock are among the first birds to move in as the forest starts to regenerate. Aspen grow from sucker plants off the roots of the parent tree. To inhibit competition, the parent tree chemically suppresses the growth of these suckers while it is alive, but once it is felled, the suckers take off and grow at an astounding rate—up to one inch a day at peak growing times. Within a couple of years, depending on soil fertility, moisture, sunlight, and the quality of the now-cut parent trees, there can be up to 40,000 small aspen trees per acre on a clearcut. These small trees shade out the thick grasses the woodcock dislike, yet they provide the overhead cover they desire. Many times the birds will do their spring singing right on a bare patch of earth that the timbering equipment chewed up during logging.

Clearcutting is becoming more acceptable as time goes along and the results of the operation become observable. But still, because a fresh clearcut looks like a fresh nuclear attack site, there are those who are opposed to the practice for esthetic reasons. Such folks are normally not bird hunters.

As a clearcut ages, some trees compete more effectively and survive, shading out the weaker or less lucky trees. This process, in turn, allows the trees that survive to grow faster, continuing to shade out the slower-growing trees. The attrition thus continues at a steady pace.

Eventually, the forest, instead of comprising tens of thousands of small aspen, is made up of just dozens of very big aspens. These are no good for woodcock cover—or any kind of cover at all—and are really only good for ruffed grouse, which "bud" on them as their main source of winter food.

So in order to regenerate an aspen forest, the cutting has to be done while there are still aspen present, before red maple, oaks, or other trees of later stages displace the aspen. The large aspens have to be cut while the root suckers still live, dormant, on the parent tree. Once the aspen ecosystem has passed into the next stage of forest development, it is hard to get the stem densities through clearcutting that aspen will otherwise provide.

Enlightened game departments regularly use clearcutting as a method of managing habitat for grouse, deer, and other wildlife of the early successional stage. Woodcock are rarely considered the primary beneficiary of such cutting, but they benefit nonetheless.

Land Management

The future of woodcock shooting is tied, then, to the future of land management. God only made so much land, but apparently he hasn't decided how many people he's going to make, so as populations swell and land becomes less available, the land that is left has to be intensively managed for specific purposes.

Those who have the idea that woodcock cover can be among those specific purposes can take up a chainsaw, the modern forest-management tool.

Game departments are probably equipped to do it better, but if you have land available to you, you can do your own woodcock (and ruffed grouse and deer) management. With the private control of land for hunting becoming more prevalent, we all want to be a little more actively involved in how the land is maintained.

In parts of the country private use of land on a restricted basis is a way of life; if you don't have a shooting lease in Texas, for example, you won't do much hunting unless you have friends who have leases. On the Great Plains, more and more pheasant land is turning to hunt-for-pay, the harbinger of leased land, which clearly seems to be in the future in the more popular areas.

In woodcock range there are areas where clubs and individuals have tied up tracts for hunting, and more of this is taking place each year. There will always be open areas, but with private ownership starting to rear its head, you may be inclined to lease, rent, or buy land for woodcock hunting. If so, you should know that there are ways you can improve it.

Land that has aspen on it, even mature aspen, is the best land. If the area has a stream course, riverbed, or natural passage between hills, benches, or mountains, you have some potentially good land. Naturally, I assume you will get this land in an area that woodcock are using—it won't be in Arizona, for example.

One of the first steps is to lay out the areas you want to clearcut. These do not have to be large, although if woodcock are to be managed along with grouse, you may want to make them a bit larger. The grouse need larger areas because they use the habitat yearlong and they need it in varying age classes to fulfill their life cycles successfully.

But on the average, two or three acres of aspen will yield good cover when treated properly. This treatment consists of going into an area, laying out the boundaries of the cut (irregular to take advantage of natural land formations), and dropping everything—*everything*—onto the ground. The area will look totally denuded if you've done it right. Don't spare solitary pine trees; such trees are hiding spots for goshawks, one of the worst predators on grouse and other gamebirds.

The cut will start to regenerate very quickly. Aspen suckers will sprout off the roots of the downed trees within a year of the cutting, and within three years the woodcock will start using the area for resting cover. These first aspens (either quaking aspen or bigtooth aspen) will have huge shade leaves to better capture the sun for food making. The leaves are also quite frost resistant, meaning they will stay on later into the fall, offering even better cover to flighting woodcock.

Within six or seven years, perhaps fewer, ruffed grouse will start using the cut for drumming and for cover as well. But we aren't going to wait around for the woodcock and grouse to use this place. A cut should be made every other year or perhaps every third year until your entire land, wherever applicable, is checkerboarded. That way you will always have areas in prime and other areas coming into prime.

Normally, the cuts will stay prime for something less than a decade, so you must have spots always on their way to becoming good, huntable cover. By the time you have done your work in four or five areas of your land, the original cut will have become old and will need cutting again. Then you simply rotate areas that have already been cut and cut them again as the years pass.

Leaving areas bare (hauling off the logs and brush) can create places the males will use for singing, and if you have picked a higher area overlooking a stream with some alder present, you may just have created your own Valhalla for woodcock.

2

The Cabin: A Diary

Day 1

I drove the seven hours and one time zone northwest through a rain that didn't stop for two minutes the whole way. The colors were starting to show up when I took the time to notice, but the drizzle made both them and me dull, and so mostly I watched the road. I stopped and ate—something—at noon. At one in the afternoon, I turned onto the two-lane blacktop of a county road to make the last fifty miles of the trip to The Cabin.

There are places without names, but up here there are names with no places to go with them. This country is dotted with them. They were once towns, then whistle stops, and now they are just names awaiting their return to the wilderness, when the forest will wash over them like a wave washing over a sand castle, built then forgotten by a fickle child. A few years from now a summer-intern mapmaker down at the state capitol will see some of those names, shrug, and then black-line them into historical purgatory. Once the lumbermen who cut the great trees left, there was little to keep those who followed the camps, and finally only the sign names were left. Each autumn the signs lean a little more, and some year they will topple, and the mark of many dead citizens who lived and loved here will fall to the ground as well.

The Cabin looks the same. It's been waiting for me for a year. The little lake that lives next to The Cabin is speckled with raindrops and has started to dress itself in autumn finery. The red and yellow maples dance with the green spruces to the tune of a freshening breeze on the far shore. I smile at the lake.

The first time I saw it, the little lake was whooping it up with a gale that could have blown the lights out of a freighter on the Big Lake. The Cabin shuddered that night, and I lay awake wondering if we both were going to slide down the hill. But we didn't, and the lake has been a docile mistress ever since.

Brown Car slides to a halt and I back up to the door. Brown Car is my station wagon and pal. He lets me sleep inside him sometimes, and he gets me where I'm going. His odometer says a hundred grand and counting, but he runs like a sewing machine and doesn't have a dab of rust. The guys must have made him after deer season and they all got bucks, because he doesn't have any rust—none. Brown Car could get to The Cabin alone if I gave him his keys.

Jess, my setter, whines. Dogs are either too dumb or too smart for their own good. I think dumb is better because Jess is the opposite. She runs inside The Cabin and stands up at the sink, asking for a drink. I give her one, and she starts looking for Chris, my older son. He isn't there, as he has been in the past, because he is now in high school and high schools have no sense of humor about kids taking the second week of school off to go woodcock hunting. I wish he were here, too, because now I have to unload all the stuff myself.

And I miss him. Next year, when he is older and it is legal, Jake, my younger son, will be here. But this year I am alone.

When you're alone, you have to do everything right then because otherwise it piles up. I unload the kitchen stuff, put the perishables into the refrigerator, and then unpack my gear.

The gun comes in first. My Parker sixteen-gauge in its leg-o-mutton case, then the vests and hats and boots and shells and the rest of it.

The weather has started to clear, so Jess and I decide that we should hunt. We head for a covert we call "Dawson" (as in Robert Service's "Over the Dawson Trail") and find that the puddles on the two-track are too deep. Brown Car is willing, but I pull rank and park. We walk for a half-hour on the flooded track, hunt ten minutes, and Jess makes a half-assed point on a woodcock. The bird chooses the only direction I can see to shoot, and I dump him at fifteen yards. We walk out and head home, where I hang the bird from the bird straps on the front porch. I let woodcock hang for a day before I clean them, taking down, say, Monday's birds on Tuesday and cleaning them when I hang Tuesday's birds.

The sky is clear and the geese are singing in the swamp beyond the lake as Jess and I fix a drink and walk down to the lake at sunset. The Scotch tastes good. The summer has been hectic, but now autumn's here, and I have a full schedule of fun. I finish the drink and walk back up the hill to make dinner—nothing fancy, just some warmed-up stew I smuggled out of the house with me. I drive the thirteen miles to the phone to call home. I talk with everyone, and they are happy I'm okay. They take me in stride. For ten months out of the year I do all the right things. I coach baseball and basketball teams for my boys. I praise my overachiever daughter and try to con both of us into believing I'm still smarter than she is. I go to PTA meetings and school conferences. And I pretend I'm awake during church sermons.

But in the fall I turn into a vagrant. I hit the road. They know this and understand. A week and a half ago, I was in

Mexico shooting at whitewings. Now I'm at The Cabin waiting for the frost to come. Next month, somewhere else—and the next. But autumn doesn't start until I've had my time at The Cabin, and that's now. I turn in after I boot Jess off the bed.

Day 2

I wake up five minutes before the clock radio comes on. I wait and listen, and pretty soon it kicks in, a local FM station with a pretty good jock named Rick who has a scam going with some character he's made up called Leon. I chuckle at it as I dress, and Rick tells us that it's *twenty-nine* degrees out. Brown Car looks like an ice cube through the window, and I slide my pants on quickly and make a huge breakfast. At home I normally have coffee and nicotine with my morning Excedrin. At the cabin I eat like a damn pig.

Jess and I get going way too early, but by nine she's pointed six woodcock, and I have one. I've missed some and didn't see the rest. Woodcock can slicker one man and one dog in thick cover. They have too many choices. But later I take another on a hard right-hander, debate about counting my shells to figure my shooting average, and can the idea. At the end of a season I'll end up three birds per five shells. Some say they never miss. Must be they never miss when I'm not with them. Three out of five has been my tally for twenty years. Won't get any better, and I hope it doesn't get any worse.

Jess and I sit on Brown Car's tailgate eating candy bars. The leaves are flittering down from the frost, and the sky is so blue it hurts to look at it. I laugh out loud at myself. I have my Parker and my orange belton setter and my station wagon and I have on my vest and brush pants and weathered boots and my pipe and my primpy little tweed hat with the pins that show I know how to pay dues. I am a living cliché. I don't know if I love it or hate it.

The day rolls along, and toward evening I drive the

twenty back-road miles to the grocery store and buy a steak and some stew meat. Standing in line, I hear a voice telling another voice about the best way to kill deer. Seems, says Voice No. 1, you soak carrots in salt brine for a week and then dump the carrots near your stand. Voice No. 2 marvels at the ploy. Voice No. 1, whom I have now dubbed, silently, "The Cretin," haw-haws about how deer will stay right there while he shoots at them with his bow and arrows. I sneak a peak at The Cretin and my opinion is vindicated: beady eyes, a beard that looks like a cherry bomb in a roll of steel wool, and a Massey-Ferguson hat. One of the area's local outlaws.

The check-out girl nervously looks from me to The Cretin because by now he and I have silently decided to hate each other, and she asks me quickly if the stew meat is for me or my dog—somehow she knows my dog is the one sitting in the driver's seat of the station wagon in the lot out there. I lie and tell her it's for the dog and then decide to give Jess my stew meat after all. She isn't *that* fat. The Cretin is trying to talk to the girl over my shoulder and I can see her skin crawl.

I pay for my stuff and leave and The Cretin follows, telling Voice No. 2 about all the deer he is going to *kill*, with the emphasis there for my benefit. I open the back of the wagon and put the sack in as The Cretin roars away in a '64 Chevy—heading away from the way I'm going. I breathe easy.

Driving back at twilight, we are at the breakneck speed of twenty-five when Brown Car stands on his nose. There is a nice buck in the road, watching us. The buck ambles off into the roadside cover and is gone, and I wonder if The Cretin will have any luck against deer like that one. The deer's eyes showed more fire and intelligence than The Cretin's, so I'm betting on the deer.

I hear a rustling in the back, and Jess is eating the stew meat already. I holler at her to leave my steak alone, and she grudgingly stops. That's dogs: genes and bloodlines better than mine, and she's a damn bag lady after one day at The Cabin.

The steak—my half, anyway—was delicious. So was the

Scotch and my after-dark pipe by the lake. Swell—a strange male dog ambles up and sniffs Jess. She's probably coming into heat because she hands this mutt his head and he seems to like it. I cluck her inside for the night.

Day 3

I awake to rain. It almost always rains for a day or two at The Cabin. I use the time to sleep, listen to Rick, catch up on some reading, play with Jess—who is by now tired enough that I wonder if she'll bite me if I get too frisky with her. She *is* in heat, and a male nondescript slides up to me when I take the garbage out to ask if she can come out and play.

Late in the day the skies dry up and the little bluegills start dimpling the lake. I hit the rack early. I'm glad it rained.

Day 4

I wait for a breeze to dry things off a bit before I start hunting. There is not the urgency that there was just a couple of days ago. The frost and the rain have thinned the cover, and now the shooting is easier. I hunt a covert I've always called "The Railroad Tracks"—because there aren't any—and I find woodcock in good numbers. It would be easy to be a hog at such times, but it is better to shoot a few birds with a few shells than many with many. Woodcock affect me like that. They are the most highly prized of all birds to me. I love the mystery they carry, I love their color and flight and their big eyes. They are autumn with wings attached. They are here so briefly that when they leave, they take the last of this season with them and bring the snow and the desolation.

Day 5

Last day. I have to head back to what passes for civilization tomorrow. Each year I hate the last day a little more. I know what waits for me back there—phone messages to be returned and work to be finished. But it is autumn, and there are other trips. I try to soothe my feelings about returning by thinking of what's ahead: Iowa for pheasants and Mississippi for quail, Ontario and the Eastern Shore for ducks and geese. But it doesn't do much good, not when you don't want to leave.

The little lake is placid this morning, so I finally unlimber my little fly rod and try for some of the stunted bluegills that live there. They are small, but I am a bad fisherman; we deserve each other. With no luck at all, I quit after a half-hour and load Brown Car. I will hunt a few last coverts today, sleep one more night at The Cabin, and leave in the morning before most decent folks are out of bed.

The first covert gives me five chances at woodcock, all over points, and a grouse Jess has bumped. I take the grouse on a lucky shot, then talk myself into believing I did it that way on purpose. I shoot one of the woodcock. Somewhere between the third and fourth woodcock flush, I get lost. I get lost every year. Once I got lost for nine hours. My compass does me no good because I have gotten complacent and didn't look at it going into the covert. Now I don't know which way out is.

The little brook I was following must have made a turn I didn't see because as far as I know, I could be in either the Yukon or an undeveloped suburb of Peoria. I am wearing a hat and boots. So far, all I know is that I am somewhere between the hat and the boots.

I start reciting the rule of threes: three minutes without air, three hours without shelter, three days without water, and three weeks without food. I decide I may not die as long as I keep breathing at regular intervals. But I sure am lost.

I stumble out onto a logging trail that leads me to a dirt road that takes me to a better dirt road that ends up being three miles from Brown Car, but I find him and everything's okay. I try to forget the panic and the rush that comes from being lost with no one to come find you. The down side of solitude is that by the time someone misses you, you could be dead.

One more covert. Two more shots. Two woodcock. Then back to The Cabin. I clean the birds and put them in the cooler for the trip home, load everything up that I can, fix a big dinner, and finish my bottle of Scotch.

The next morning The Cabin looks dark in the rear-view mirror as I pull away. "So long, friend. See you next year."

The little ripples on the little lake that lives next to The Cabin wave good-bye.

3

Woodcock Shooting

I have taken some fine shots into coverts on their first wood cock hunts. Two things strike them as unusual: first, the density of the cover—most will holler at me that as long as they're in this position, they may as well say a few Hail Marys or whatever strikes their fancy because they are spending a lot of time crawling around on their knees. The second thing that strikes them as odd is that it seems an impossible task to shoot a woodcock with anything approaching regularity. Invariably, they either don't shoot at all or they fill the air with lead at each flush, hoping by the sheer force of shot to scratch a bird down.

Getting the Hang of It

But after a while they begin to get the hang of things and the birds start to drop for them. Usually, the best woodcock shots are those who have good natural coordination. A friend of mine, Jack Morris, is a professional baseball player, one of the finest pitchers of this decade. Jack and I were hunting an alder run of about ten acres one October day, and the leaves, owing to late frosts, were still high on the trees. Jack had a no-hitter going, but it wasn't nearly as much fun as the one he threw against the White Sox in 1984. He cursed the cover and his little twenty-eight-gauge double. Finally, I told him to just look at the bird and shoot—forget about swing and lead, just let his natural coordination take over. The birds started to come down.

There are some who are not meant to be good woodcock shooters, I'm convinced. If you've been reared on pheasants and full chokes or ducks over decoys, the speed adjustments are often too great. You'll get there if you give it long enough, but most of the time discouragement sets in and you lose interest. The shooting of a woodcock on most days and in most coverts is a fast proposition. There is almost always more time than you think, but when you go for the bird, everything has to come together quickly or it won't come together at all. The mount, the abbreviated swing, and the triggering of the shot from an experienced woodcock hunter seem to be all in one blurred motion, and often they are.

But still more often there is time for adjustment, and the adjustment comes quickly if you stay at it. I think that woodcock shooters are more paranoid about their shooting than anyone except maybe quail hunters, another reflection on the traditionalist mentality these sports seem to foster. I used to keep track—scrupulously—of the number of birds I shot compared with the shells I touched off doing it. After ten years it became obvious that not much was going to change, so I quit, and I enjoy myself more now. If I used to get three birds with as many shells, I started dreading a point from my dog because it became an opportunity to end my little mini-streak.

Over those ten years I found that I shot about 60 percent—three birds with five shells, not three birds in five opportunities. If you need to know how well you shoot, I can

One of the best places for woodcock—second-growth alder that is pioneering what was once pastureland. Quite often, woodcock will hold just inside the edges of such places, especially when they are close to feeding cover and are using the alders for resting cover during the daylight hours. Then, the birds will cross the open land and settle in the first available cover for the day, the alder edge.

tell you that if you hit half of the birds you fire at and count each shell, you've got nothing to be ashamed of. That's over a good dog in thick cover. Some days you won't hit any.

There are times when woodcock can be brutally easy, say when a flight has come in the night before and the birds are tired. Then they twitter up feebly and you can make a long run if you're so inclined. On such days, shoot a bird or two, but then put away the gun and take the chance to work your dog—and give the birds their lives. It's like throwing back a trout after you've caught him.

Fine Guns for Fine Game

Most of the woodcock hunters I know spend more time trying to get just the right gun than any other batch of upland shooters I can think of. I'm counting right now, and I can remember that I have had fourteen "perfect" woodcock guns, guns I was sure would make me a legend. I'll probably stick with the latest one because I've used it for three years now—something of a record for me—and it's done well.

As you know, there are several actions of guns, and everyone has his preferences. I've read, "The best gun for woodcock is the one you can hit woodcock with," and this is true to a point, but that's like saying, "The best car is the one that runs." There are elements of style, grace, pride of ownership, and economy to be taken into account with both cars and guns.

Hunting woodcock is addicting because it is fun. The birds are among the most interesting of all creatures and we are out after them at the finest time of year amid the most beautiful colors found anywhere on earth. Nobody is going to stay alive on the woodcock he brings to bag, so here we make adjustments in our way of choosing guns.

What I'm saying is this: A woodcock is a bird of mystery and of upland-shooting tradition, to northerners what the bobwhite is to southerners. Why not carry a gun you can be proud of?

Let's take a look. The pump action shotgun is, like its

mechanized cousin the autoloader, a gun whose balance and handling characteristics are better suited to other tasks, like shooting ducks and geese. It does not carry well because of the magazine tube, and it does not come up handily and easily because of the action, which adds several inches of steel to the length of the gun. I have pumps and autos, and I use them for duck hunting, where I don't have to carry them far or often. Repeating shotguns are not for woodcock hunting—they are wrong practically and esthetically.

Instead, the woodcock hunter is better served by a double. There are several reasons.

First, the opportunity to shoot three times at woodcock without reloading is virtually nonexistent. I have never shot a double on woodcock, and I know a lot of hunters in the same boat. I know men who have shot back-to-back singles and then wrote in for their Orvis Doubles Pins, but these aren't true doubles, in which both birds are in flight before Our Hero goes to work on the first one. When shooting at a single woodcock, the chance to fire more than two shots is rare, and if it does present itself, the third shot is usually a long drag at a bird topping out over the trees. So much for firepower.

The double, either over–under or side by side, is the choice of those who spend a lot of time in the woods, and not just for the sake of tradition, either. Lately the market for high-grade guns with two barrels has increased dramatically. At the same time the market for repeating guns has fallen off. Americans are in a state of upland-hunting transition, a switch from the era of big bags and repeating guns to one in which the value is placed on the experience.

Evolution of a Hunter

Studies have shown that a hunter goes through several stages in his development. First, he is an inept but eager youngster, intent on learning all he can and spending as much time as possible hunting. He isn't very good, his bags are small, he often hunts with a buddy or two, and groups are common. He rarely has a dog, and if he does, the dog is rarely any good—probably also rarely in sight. He spends a good portion of his time hunting anything that comes along. On a typical day he may take shots at grouse, woodcock, pheasants, rabbits, and a stray wood duck he flushed off a pond. Most of the time he hunts lousy cover because he isn't yet sure what good cover looks like.

Later, as he gains knowledge and skill, he enters the stage called "collector." He gets really good at judging cover, finding birds, and shooting them. There is little wasted motion as he goes about his business of killing birds. He does it quickly and efficiently with the limit his goal. Often he is disappointed if he comes up short. He equates his skill at taking a limit of game with his manhood or something or other: He has a drive to succeed, and his success, to him, is measured in his bag. It takes a number of such successes before he moves on to the stage at which the experience of hunting itself is the attraction.

At this final stage, the "experience" stage, Our Pal has nothing left to prove. Sure, he'd like to shoot a bird or two—that's why he's there—but if he doesn't take his limit, it won't matter to him. In some cases he will end the day while there are still birds to be shot right in front of him. Like a trout fisherman who starts throwing back his catch, he starts to have a different definition of a successful hunt.

My two sons are woodcock hunters. The older lad, Chris, is sixteen and has become a nearly perfect woodcock hunter. He is young, well coordinated, an excellent shot, and he has enough drive to go all day. When he was younger, it was really important for him to shoot a lot of birds, or at least to do a lot of shooting. He shot woodcock with me many days when I didn't fire a shot, and he started to wonder about my desire to hunt—was I out there just for him? What's the deal here?

Because of the business I'm in—hunting and writing about it—Chris got to go a lot of places with me and shoot a lot of different kinds of game, so he started to move into the "experience" stage sooner than most, and now shooting a

Author's son, Chris, goes into action on a 'cock flushed from streamside cover in the early season. This is not an unusual shot, but it is often missed because the bird will normally curve out and then back in toward cover, offering what appears to be a straightaway shot, but which isn't. This is a good place, however, to position young shooters or beginners because the shots are normally fairly open and there is some chance of success. Note how the setter in the foreground, having pointed the bird, is holding steady to wing; steady to shot is another matter.

limit is not as important as it once was. The dog work, the crystal sky—these are the things that matter.

My younger son, Jason, is thirteen and has hunted woodcock only one year. He's still trying to figure out how to hit them, and he is not yet ready to be called a "collector." He hunts with us, so he gets good dog work in good cover and he gets a lot of chances. His coordination is excellent also, and a few birds have fallen, but not enough to take the edge off. In a few years, maybe.

I know a fellow in his thirties who talks wonderfully about the experience of woodcock hunting and the fine guns and the finer days and the classic dog work. In the coverts he'll bowl you over getting to the dog before you when she points. He, like my younger son, has not evolved to the point where he can appreciate woodcock for something other than a tricky target. His hunting experience is limited, and it shows. Moving from stage to stage is a function of the number of times you hunt, and this eager-beaver type shows himself to be inexperienced, his Scotch-whiskey talk notwithstanding. Nothing against him, mind you, it's just that he's not yet *there*.

So it is with guns. As young beginners, we usually take what's handed to us into the woods. As we get older and save a few bucks, we are able to afford our own guns and so we usually go with the most shots per dollar and spring for a repeater—a pump or auto, normally in twelve gauge. It seems like a good bargain for hunting everything, and it is.

But for the woodcock specialist, the one who hunts little or nothing else as long as the birds are in the coverts, a gun for everything doesn't make sense. So as we move to the experience stage, we usually choose a double because it is more in keeping with our new-found appreciation of the nuances, the finer things that fit together to make each day something to be remembered.

This long story leads me to the point I want to make: I think that entire hunting populations go through the same developmental stages that hunters as individuals go through. Back in the 1940s, when birds were maybe more plentiful and the rooster pheasant was king across much of America, we were a nation of collectors, intent on full game bags, and we knew how to do it. But as that species' numbers dropped off, we turned elsewhere, and many of us turned to woodcock.

We aged: The hunting population, reflecting the demographics of the country, also aged, and we moved to the next stage of development as a group. We are becoming decidedly more British or European in our outlook on things like guns and gear and the gadgets we use while hunting. If you doubt it, take a look at the offerings in some of the upper-crust outdoor catalogs we all get each fall from places like Orvis or Dunn's or Old Guide. Who would have thought twenty-five years ago that there would ever be a strong market for British thornproof oiled-cotton hunting coats at $180 a copy? We would have scoffed then; today we buy them.

So our choices of guns have changed. We no longer seek the guns we did as collectors—autoloaders and pumps—but are interested in guns we can be proud of all year. That has shown itself, through market studies and sales figures, to be the double.

Side-by-Side Specifics

The over–under is a fine gun. It has balance, style, and for those who like it, a single sighting plane. It has two chokes available, and many are now made with screw-in choke devices so you can make it shoot almost any way you want it to. It is respectable to carry as well.

But it has its drawbacks. First, it is a trifle heavy. Compared with the stock dimensions and barrel lengths of a side-by-side double, it will run about a half-pound more. As a result most over–unders you see in the woodcock coverts are small-gauge guns: twenties and twenty-eights.

Another drawback, in my opinion, *is* the single sighting plane. In the woods that narrow rib is often lost against the background of poor light and thick foliage that so often marks a woodcock shot. I think that if you quizzed over–under users, you'd find in most cases that the last gun they

This woodcock hunter has chosen a light twenty-eight-gauge side-by-side double for his work on early-season woodcock. When leaves are on the trees and shots are close, nothing handles as fast as a double, but the ultralight gun can sometimes be over-twitchy, making for fast mounts but unsteady shooting. The best woodcock gun is a well-balanced one with the ballistic efficiency to handle the fragile birds. The twenty-eight suffices for many shooters.

used was either a pump or an autoloader, and that the over–under presented a sight picture to them that they were familiar with. To many this is a decided aid.

But some of us actually like the wide sighting plane of a side-by-side double. The rib, especially a swamped rib that funnels the eye down between the barrels, helps in the vertical, up-and-down pointing that characterizes woodcock shots. When I go after a rising woodcock, the wide barrels give me the impression of a floor coming up after the bird. There is no mystery where the barrels are or where they are pointing because they are so easy to see, even if peripherally, as I try to focus on the bird.

Additionally, the side by side is normally a lighter gun, the bolting mechanisms being less bulky than on an over–under. This weight savings gives you an advantage not in handling speed but in carrying weight, measurable at the end of a long day. The side by side can easily be carried in one hand while you unwrap grapevines from around your neck with the other. In a pinch a well-balanced side by side can be tossed to your shoulder with one hand for a shot.

Made in England and Europe

Of the side by sides, the best are those that were made in England and Europe between the two world wars. Of these, the classic sidelock guns turned out one at a time in London are considered the best, with those from Birmingham, England, a close second. The fit, the finish, the engraving, the checkering — all are first-class. These guns are virtually indestructible as well, and on the used-gun market they command premium prices.

Additionally, they can be made — and were made — to very light weights. An American used to American guns may pride himself on his six-pound, twenty-gauge over–under bird gun — until he handles a twelve-gauge British gun of the same weight with balance that makes it faster than his twenty. Then lights start to go on and bank balances drop.

For example, a gun I have is a sixteen-gauge, a boxlock of

Getting ready to work a patch of young aspen off logging trails in Michigan's Upper Peninsula. This hunter favors a twenty-eight but is using a handguard to enlarge the feel of the double's slim barrels. The aspen cover shown is the result of regeneration of the forest after clearcutting. Forestry practices, especially those where pulpwood is cut for paper companies, provide excellent cover.

best grade for this style, made in London in 1920. With twenty-eight-inch barrels, it weighs exactly five and a half pounds, about the weight of an American-made twenty-eight-gauge side by side and less than a twenty-eight-gauge over–under.

The reason for this is that American gunmakers have for years labored under some hindrances that the Europeans have not had to cope with. American guns often had to be overbuilt because we lacked good repair facilities early in our history. If you were going into the wilderness with a gun, you didn't want it to break on you 200 miles by foot trail from the nearest gunsmith. So all parts were built bigger and heavier than they had to be.

Second, the Europeans and British have proof houses, where the government certifies the gun to be safe by firing heavy proof loads through it. If the thing doesn't fly apart, it's okay to be sold. America has no proof houses. If a gun doesn't stand up under the rigors of firing and something happens to it that could injure the shooter, there is no government agency to take the heat—it falls directly on the manufacturer, and we all know what product-liability suits are these days. So it is in the American maker's best financial interest to overbuild guns, even today.

In Europe, where proof houses have existed for many decades, the gunmaker is free to use light yet extremely strong steels and to shave each excess ounce during the making of a fine game gun, ounces that add up to pounds over comparable American shotguns.

James Purdey & Sons of London, probably the most renowned name in gunmaking, lists its twelve-gauge gun, a sidelock chambered for the 2¾-inch shell, at six and a half pounds. It lists its twelve-gauge sidelock chambered for the British 2½-inch shell (cartridge) at an even six pounds with twenty-six-inch barrels—the weight of a very light American over–under twenty-gauge. As you'd guess, the weights are progressively less for Purdeys of smaller gauge. As a matter of fact, whenever a gun of this quality is made by any of the world's fine makers, weight—within reason—is one of the "bespoke," or custom, elements the purchaser can specify.

Europeans are accustomed to shooting smaller shot charges than are Americans. A normal shot load from a twelve-gauge in England is only one and one-sixteenth ounces, and the twenty is used to throw seven-eighths ounce of shot instead of the traditional full-ounce American load.

I have a 1932 catalog put out by Westley Richards, and it is very interesting in terms of the guns the English firm offered during that Golden Age. There were best-grade side-locks, to be sure, but there were also ladies' guns and boys' guns—made lighter and in smaller gauge. How would you like to run across a five-pound, twenty-gauge side-by-side double made by Westley Richards right now? The firm's offerings went up through huge doubles, intended for water-fowl, that were four-gauge and weighed up to twenty-four pounds! That's quite a selection of guns, something no American company can match these days, yet Westley Rich-ards was just one of many English gunmakers plying the trade between the wars.

Gauge

This leads to a look, in a roundabout way, at the question of gauge itself. So often, gauge is discussed from the stand-point of gun weight. Does a hunter want a twenty because he likes the twenty-gauge—its ballistics, its shot load, its choice of shot sizes—or because he likes the weight and size that a twenty-gauge gun normally presents?

European guns offer larger gauges with near-American twenty-gauge weight and handling characteristics. If the average woodcock hunter were acquainted with these, would he think that a sixteen or a twelve would do just as well? Let's see.

A gun kills because of the shot size it throws, the amount of shot it throws, and the pattern efficiency, or way it throws (uniformity, spread, and shortness of the shot string). To get the gun into the position where it has a chance to perform is a function of the gun's handling characteristics—weight, but more important the balance and the arrangement of the hands on the plane the shot travels. Add to this the fit of the stock and how well the shooter likes his gun, and you have a nearly total package.

The twenty-gauge, which seems to be the standard woodcock gauge of choice, is normally used in the woodcock coverts with one ounce of shot, sometimes a bit less (seven-eighths-ounce skeet loads), but rarely more. This gauge offers a wide variety of loads with varying powder charges and shot sizes in the one-ounce configuration. In upland hunting (and universally with woodcock) there is little reason to use anything more than an ounce of shot, the exceptions being pheasants or other big tough birds, such as prairie grouse of the various species.

But the woodcock is neither big nor tough. For years I shot woodcock with a twenty and seven-eighth-ounce No. 9 skeet loads; market hunters used No. 10s and smaller when they could get them. In their cylinder-barrel brush guns an ounce of 10s must have delivered a terrific pattern, although they seldom used even half that amount.

So if we say that an ounce of shot is the maximum for woodcock and less certainly wouldn't hurt, then we have to start looking at woodcock guns in terms of their capacity to handle this amount of shot rather than by gauge.

The twenty has what woodcock hunters need: good handling, light weight, ability to handle an ounce of shot or a bit less, and all tied up in a package that is fun to own and carry. But other gauges can do the job as well. Let's take a look at the twenty-eight gauge, a bore gaining in popularity. The twenty-eight's allure comes from a few sources. One is its lighter weight, which makes it easier to carry—it's lighter than the twenty in most cases. Second, the standard three-fourths-ounce shot load of the twenty-eight is fast moving, and in skeet (No. 9) configuration it is quite deadly. It has been said that the twenty-eight-gauge kills like a twenty, its shot string being shorter and therefore harder hitting because more of the shot arrives on target together, maximizing hitting power. I have shot many woodcock with a twenty-eight and I agree; a twenty-eight makes the brown feathers fly. It has less recoil than a twenty shooting a standard load, and—maybe the most important feature—there are a lot of nifty little side by sides being imported right now in twenty-eight gauge. These guns possess the feel of the twenty without the toyness of the .410, yet they can be carried in one hand and come into play quickly because there is enough gun to build in handling qualities in the design. I sometimes do my woodcock hunting, especially in the early season, with a twenty-eight-gauge sidelock.

Alas, the twenty-eight isn't exactly standard equipment in a lot of woodcock states, so the shells aren't readily available. Those that are available are usually in No. 7½ or larger. A good rule is that when you are shooting No. 7½ shot or bigger, you have to increase the size of the shot load to keep pellet count up where it belongs. You may be able to get by with, say, an ounce of No. 7½ for a certain purpose, but if you have to go to No. 6, you'd better have one and one-eighth ounces or the pattern will get too thin. The alternative is to go to tighter chokes, and then hitting suffers. More on chokes in a bit.

So if I were going to use a twenty-eight on woodcock, I'd stick with No. 9 skeet loads and also stick to conservative shots—shots at birds well within range—and pass up anything that tops out over the trees at thirty-five yards. In fact, that's good advice no matter what you're shooting. By the way, here's something interesting: The three-fourth-ounce twenty-eight gauge skeet load (No. 9 shot) contains 439 shot; a full ounce of No. 8 contains 410 shot.

Unless you hand load, the twenty-eight does not have the flexibility of the twenty—you can't get shot loads of more than three-fourths of an ounce, another somewhat limiting factor. That may change. Federal once made a one-ounce, twenty-eight-gauge magnum load for use on bigger birds, but the load died because few people shot a twenty-eight.

The .410 is often thought of as a woodcock gun, and in the hands of some people it may well be. But I can't in good conscience recommend it for anyone under any conditions for woodcock. It strings shot badly, patterns poorly, and is a crippler in the worst sense. To be sporting, you must give this fine bird its due, and needlessly crippling birds for the sake of so-called "sportsmanship" when you mean "challenge" is wrong. You are there to kill birds—never forget that. Save your challenges for the skeet field, where a nicked target will not suffer.

What about the twelve-gauge, the standard British game-shooting gauge? Does it have a place in the woodcock coverts? What are the criteria? Will it shoot an ounce of shot? Yes—there are some nice light one-ounce loads available from all the ammunition companies, including light one-ounce target loads. In addition, some imported shells like the Eley cartridge from England can be had in 2½-inch length, and they carry just a tad over an ounce of shot; in 2-inch shells, the shot load is a shade under an ounce.

A friend of mine, Doug Brunson, claims the 2-inch twelve-gauge is a fine upland gun for use on such birds as grouse, woodcock, and quail. He says the 2-inch shell patterns its ounce (or thereabouts) of shot better than almost anything because of the wider bore diameter of the twelve. Doug's thinking parallels that of the British, who use the same gauge—the twelve—for all birds but change shot loads as the situation dictates.

What about weight? I can't think of an American twelve with woodcock-hunting weight, but there are a lot of imported guns that fall between five and a half pounds and six and a half pounds, a category suitable for most folks for woodcock. Some of these are cheap Spanish guns; others are fifty-year-old London Best guns that'll clean you out. Both handle the same as lighter guns, especially the better ones, because there is something about the balance and the fit that makes them fast, even if their weight is a bit more than you'd like. I see nothing wrong with shooting woodcock with a light twelve-gauge that is shooting light loads. Anyone who gives you a hard time about it doesn't know his guns.

The Sixteen

The last gauge is my favorite, a dinosaur, a throwback to when kids shot twenties and duck hunters shot twelves and *real* bird hunters shot . . . sixteens. I shoot a sixteen-gauge at woodcock and almost everything else these days. It's a low-grade Parker made in 1927, America's "last happy year," but it is fitted for me and I love it. Last season, changing just shot sizes, I shot woodcock, ruffed grouse, pheasants, quail, doves, and ducks over decoys (in Canada) with this gun. I shot it pretty well because I was shooting it a lot and not switching guns around for once in my life.

I think that the sixteen is like the twenty-eight in that it handles its shot load well for the length of the shot column and the bore diameter of the barrel. The sixteen was designed, after all, for one ounce of shot. When skeet was shot with a sixteen years back, the legal load was one ounce of shot.

The sixteen has had some problems since its heyday of the 1930s, when it was at its peak. In the South the sixteen was *the* quail hunter's gun, and in the North, by some accounts, the sixteen probably took more grouse and woodcock than any other gauge. This was the age of the Parker, the Ithaca, the Smith, the Lefever, and others.

The often-heard praise of the sixteen was that it "carried like a twenty but shot like a twelve." To a great degree this was true. Each gun was built on a frame made for it, between the twentys and the twelves, and weights were right between these other two bores.

But then along came the twenty-gauge resurgence, its loads enlarged, and the sixteen started to fall from favor. Why carry a heavier gun when a light twenty would shoot an ounce of shot? If you wanted more than an ounce, you probably wanted a twelve anyway, and even if you didn't, there was a 3-inch twenty that would hold almost one and a quarter (later exactly one and a quarter) ounces of shot.

Then the gunmakers stopped making a sixteen that *was* a sixteen. Instead, they built the guns on twelve-gauge frames and thus saddled the shooter with twelve-gauge weight. Eventually, hunters followed like cattle in this marketing direction, rather than insisting that gunmakers do things up right.

But there are two sources for real sixteens. The first is the imported gun market. The sixteen is still strong on the continent of Europe—Germany especially—and is also made by a number of Spanish firms that seem to be making guns better and better these days. The other source is the used-gun market, through which I got my Parker. If you look over the offerings of places that specialize in fine guns, you'll find a number of not only European guns, but also Parkers, Smiths, and others in sixteen gauge.

These are guns that may be fifty or sixty years old, but they are still sound because they were made well, and they were made before all that sixteen-on-a-twelve-frame business came about. Almost universally, such guns are found at lower prices than comparable models in twenty and twelve. Sometimes the price difference is staggering, with a classic sixteen from the old days selling for what an out-of-the-box over–under twenty would sell for today—and in my opinion, it's twice the gun.

Using light No. 8s (with two and a half drams of powder), the sixteen shoots nicely with little recoil. Its balance is superb in the better makes, and some can be unbelievably light, like the five-and-a-half-pounder I mentioned earlier in this chapter. Although they don't readily advertise it, some of the best and most famous game shots in this country prefer a sixteen over all others. One fine shot of my acquaintance does all his shooting with twelves, sixteens, and twenty-eights; he doesn't even own a twenty!

Weight

Now that the matter of gauge has been sufficiently confused, let's take a look at weight. I've mentioned five and a half to six and a half as being perfect for most people, but some folks do better with light guns, others with heavier. A light gun causes some people to stop the swing and shoot behind, whereas others find a heavy gun too slow in coming into play.

Here is a test you can use to judge the weight best for you: Grasp your gun (empty) or one you're considering buying by the grip, one-handed, with the gun pointed toward the ground alongside you. Then, still one-handed, raise it to shooting position, pointing up at about a forty-five-degree angle. Slowly turn in a circle, still holding the gun in shooting position with one hand. If you can do this, your gun isn't too heavy for you. If you can't, it weighs too much.

But weight is relative. If you're a six-foot two-inch rough-in carpenter, seven and a half pounds may feel light; if you're scrawny and push pencils around for a living, five and a half pounds may be right.

Balance

Balance is also important when considering weight. A well-balanced woodcock gun will come up fast for almost all woodcock-shooting situations regardless of weight. I think of balance first rather than weight, the same way I think of effective shot load before gauge.

In the thick stuff, where we often carry the gun by the grip with one hand, and on the stab-and-poke shots that woodcock offer most often, the need for a smooth-swinging gun is almost nil. Rarely do we get a chance to swing. More likely the mark is a quick flurry of wings whistling good-bye to us. We shoot by instinct and we shoot quickly or we don't shoot at all.

So woodcock shooting is unlike almost any other form of wing shooting with the exception of quail in the brush and ruffed grouse. But even these birds don't change directions the way woodcock will, and they don't float one time and bore out hard the next—they have one, wide-open speed. Woodcock have several, and sometimes you get to see all of them by the same bird in the same flight.

How should the woodcock hunter's gun be balanced?

After trying to shoot woodcock for almost thirty years, I can tell you that for me—and maybe you—a butt-heavy, muzzle-light gun is the best. This gun is virtually useless for anything out in the open, where a smooth, steady swing is needed. Instead, it is a gun that is meant to be triggered when the butt hits your shoulder and the barrels are ahead of a crossing mark or on a straightaway bird.

On a side-by-side double, or an over–under, the balance point should be to the rear of the hinge pin on which the gun pivots when you open it—approximately three inches ahead of the front trigger of a double-trigger gun. An inch to the rear of the hinge pin is about right.

Such a gun balanced this way feels lighter because the majority of the weight is handled by your triggering hand, normally a shooter's stronger hand. When a gun of average weight handles slowly and feels slow, it's usually because the weight is out front, where it has to be handled by your weaker—and extended—left hand (for a right-hander).

There are a number of ways to make a gun balance farther back, but the best seems to be to add some weight to the stock of a gun with normal, central (at the hinge pin) balance. Sometimes just the addition of a recoil pad, which weighs more than stock wood of equal size and shape, can make the difference. Other times adding lead to the hollow of a stock or boring holes and filling them with weight will do it.

One hunter I know balances his twenty-gauge by adding a slip-on recoil pad for early woodcock hunting, when he is wearing light clothing and can use the extra length in the stock. Later, when he uses this gun for other game, he takes off the recoil pad and the balance is back to normal. By that time it's usually colder, so he is wearing thicker clothing and no longer needs the extra length in the stock—it works great for him.

Barrel Length

Barrel length is a matter of some consideration. You often hear and read about short-barreled guns being the best for thick-cover shooting, but in reality it is barrel weight that matters more, assuming the gun is balanced for your work. A properly balanced gun with barrels twenty-eight inches long is not out of place in the alders: If you slap it up against a tree trying to get on a jinking woodcock, rarely is it the last two or three inches of barrel that messes you up.

But since most shotguns in the weight and gauge you probably want come with twenty-six-inch barrels, that length is just fine. Such barrels give an adequate sighting radius but still handle quickly if the rest of the gun is balanced for them. I have used from twenty-four-inch to twenty-eight-inch barrels on doubles, and I can't tell much difference in handling provided the balance point is right for me, as I explained earlier.

Stock

The stock itself should be considered carefully, both for its style and its fit. In the snapshooting situations woodcock hunters encounter, a well-fitting stock is absolutely required. It's only through long years of using a gun like this—balanced for woodcock with a stock that fits you—that you'll get really good. Even when you do, there will be days that you swear the 'cock are made of cast iron.

The stock for a woodcock gun should be straight gripped, in the English style. Pistol grips are fine, but they work against the 'cock shooter in two ways. First, they do not come into play as quickly from the positions the gun is in when a bird flushes. Forget the garbage about walking through the woods with the gun at the port-arms position. Anyone who says he can carry a gun that way all day in the unspeakable cover one has to tramp through hasn't been doing much woodcock hunting or is hunting in marginal—and open—cover. Either that or he's masochistic.

Instead, in some places you are lucky if you can get yourself through by wriggling, writhing, twisting, and turning. There is no way the gun is going to be held in the ready position all the time; the best you can do is try to have it

A high-shooting gun is what is needed for woodcock hunting, where almost all of the targets are rising. One inexpensive way to do this is to add a stick-on pad to the gun's stock. This raises the cheek, the shotgunner's rear sight, and the corresponding line of sight, which raises the point of impact. A half-pattern high at thirty yards is about right, allowing the shooter to hold above a rising bird while still being able to see the target. As shooters gain experience, they normally prefer higher stocks.

pointed in a safe direction. Besides, with a good dog the gun doesn't have to be held at the ready until the dog points.

The gun carries a bit more easily with the straight grip. If you carry the gun by the grip, fingers away from the trigger, a pistol grip kinks your wrist, a straight grip doesn't.

The straight grip allows you to start the gun toward your shoulder a bit faster than does a pistol grip. And when you have the gun mounted, the straight grip does affect your trigger hand. It throws your elbow a bit higher and thus drives your face down onto the stock, where it belongs. It also forces you to make your barrel movements more with the leading, forend hand. Tracking a bird with this hand is much easier in light of the bird's erratic flight because the muzzle-light gun moves and responds easily to the influence of the leading hand. Besides, a straight grip looks racier—and what's the matter with that?

The forend wood should be in the splinter configuration, which places both hands at the same level for faster pointing and more responsiveness. A straight grip should never be mated with a beavertail forend, nor should a pistol grip be mated with a splinter forend; the hands will be off-level with one another, and then you will have problems with vertical placement of the shot charge, especially in the excitement of a quick flush and shot. My Parker, like most Parkers, was made with a pistol grip and a splinter forend; I had the grip removed so I have the straight-grip, splinter-forend configuration I like so much.

The stock should be of the proper measurements so that it shoots high for you. The height of the comb determines how high above the rib your eye will be placed. With a side-by-side double the correct sight picture, at least for me, is to see all the barrels. It looks like I'm looking down a road, and it takes a little getting used to, but a high-shooting gun holds many advantages in the 'cock coverts.

The average shot at a woodcock is a rising shot; even birds that come out at your feet and bore away low are, in effect, rising birds. When a bird starts beneath your line of sight and flies away from you, it is flying toward the horizon.

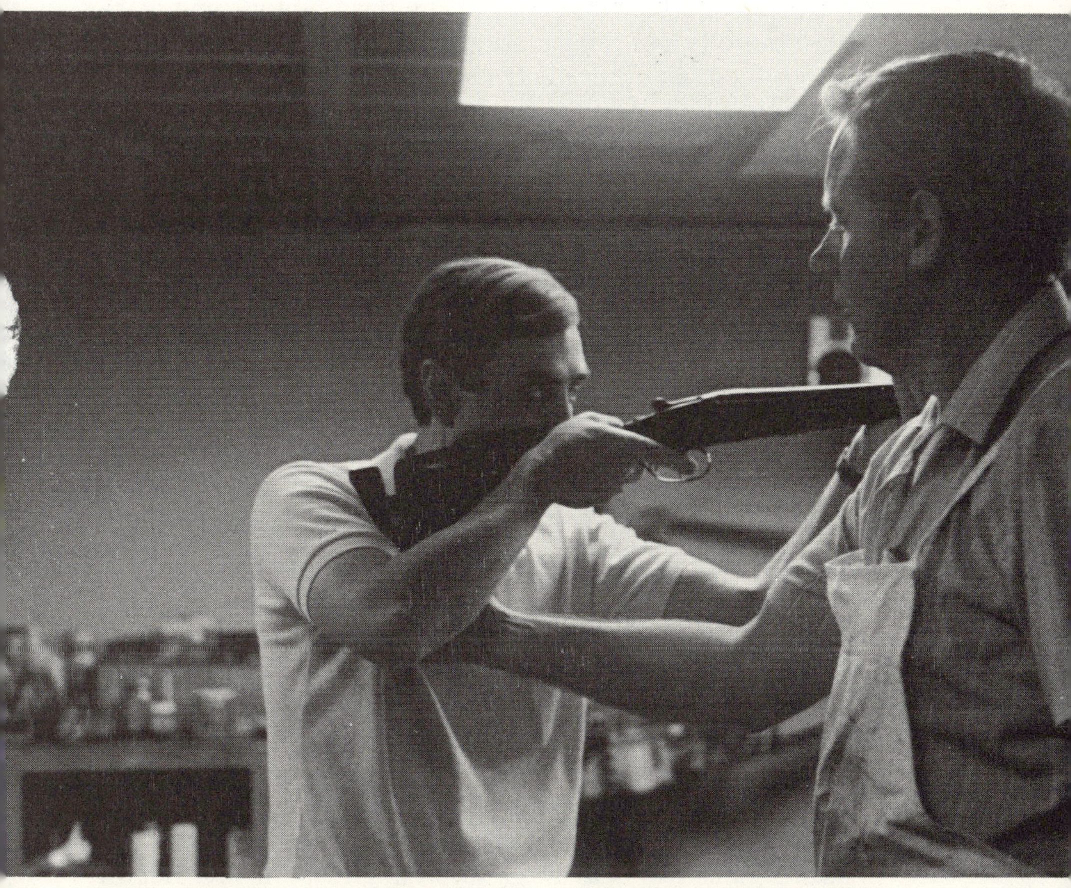

Author getting fitted for a stock by Canadian gunmaker Nicholas Makinson. The fitting is done here with a "try gun," a double with main stock parts that are moveable and thus adjustable. The main measurements are for length of pull, drop at heel, drop at comb, cast, and pitch. The straight-gripped stock is favored by many shooters because it is brought into action faster and keeps the elbow in the right position. This tends to drive the face into the gun and reduce head lifting, a main cause of misses.

So it is flying from below your eye level up to your eye level—the horizon is always at eye level.

The most common shot offered is a bird that rises almost straight up and tops the cover before heading for some place where there is less noise and a whole lot fewer people and dogs. Almost all other shots are, to one degree or another, variations of this. A high-shooting gun with little drop at the comb and heel allows you to hold nearly on the bird and the vertical lead is almost automatic.

I think most people would shoot better at all species of birds with a gun that had less drop. Face lifting is one of the most common reasons for missing, and the reason we lift our faces is because we want a really good view of the bird. With a gun stocked high, that view is possible while we are still locked into the gun—face on the stock, where it belongs.

One method of getting a higher-shooting stock is to have one whittled for you by someone who knows what he's doing and after you know what your measurements are. You may even wish to have the stock made with less drop than you think you'll need, shoot it a bit, and then have the final version carved, checkered, and finished. A stock's drop can be decreased in a variety of ways, but none are as easy as increasing the drop by sanding off a little wood from the comb.

Another way to adjust the drop is to build up the comb with something either temporary or permanent. I've used fiberglass epoxy on the comb of more than one gun. You let it harden and then sand it off and shoot it. As you might imagine, this looks like hell, and I have done it as the first step in finding my measurements, the idea being to shoot it this way for a while and then have a duplicate stock made. But with my old Parker I've been afraid to tamper, afraid that the measurements will not be accurately transferred to the new stock. So I shoot woodcock with a gun that—well—looks like hell. I get a bad time from my buddies, but I don't care. Much.

Another way to decrease the drop is through the services of a stock man who knows how to bend a stock. In this operation the grip area is heated and softened with very hot oil. Then the stock is placed in a bending jig and the pressure applied to the pliable wood until the right bend is achieved. After bending, the stock may rebound a little, so I suggest having a little more upward bend than you think you'll need to compensate for this. With older guns, made when Americans shot with their heads held higher than today (and some of those old guns had terrific amounts of comb drop), bending allows you to save and use the original wood and its attendant fine inletting and checkering. And bending is a lot cheaper than getting a new stock. The Orvis Company of Manchester, Vermont, does bending regularly and so do a lot of other places.

Choke

Now for the matter of choke. The average shot at an early-season woodcock is often measured in feet. A choke too tight will shred a bird or cause you to miss altogether. I suggest nothing tighter than improved cylinder; cylinder/improved cylinder in a gun through which you'll shoot an ounce of shot is better. With a smaller gauge or shot load, say the twenty-eight's three-fourth-ounce load, the choke should be improved cylinder/modified. A twenty, sixteen, or twelve does just fine with the cyl/ic combination.

For a lot of years I kept track of the ranges at which I actually hit woodcock. I found that year in and year out I was making first-barrel kills at about thirteen yards and second-barrel kills at fifteen or sixteen yards. This range is pure cylinder country. By the way, some of the finest-looking patterns you'll ever see are thrown by cylinder-bore guns. Modern shot cups and better powders have rendered obsolete the belief that cylinder barrels blow patterns. You still have to be on the bird, you can't shoot wildly or too fast, and you have to use caution on extralong (thirty yards or so) shots. But with a cylinder barrel and an ounce of shot, you'll do well— maybe better than you ever thought. If your reactions are a bit slower, or if your coverts offer shots longer than mine do, you may wish to tighten up. But over a dog in typical wood-cock conditions, cylinder can turn you into a legend. For example, at fifteen yards the killing pattern of a cylinder bar-rel is twenty-six inches. This means you can cleanly kill a woodcock if your hold is as much as a foot off center because there is a thirteen-inch leeway from center to edge of the killing pattern. Such a choke does not shred birds that you do center, and in the early season in thick cover fifteen yards is a typical long shot. Improved cylinder is approximately five yards tighter, throwing a twenty-inch pattern at fifteen yards and a twenty-six inch pattern at twenty yards.

Naturally, such open chokes must have their patterns made denser by smaller shot, a happy coincidence with woodcock because they are fragile birds. A skeet (No. 9) load in a twenty-gauge shell holds 512 shot, more than enough to make that twenty-six-inch pattern a deadly, dense, and *humane* tool with which to shoot woodcock.

Okay, so we agree on the gun—or else you're busy chop-ping this book into fireplace tinder. It is a double (preferably a side by side) weighing between five and a half and six and a half pounds with probably twenty-six-inch barrels. It is capa-ble of handling about an ounce of shot, and if it's anything beside a twenty-eight-gauge, it is bored cylinder/improved cylinder. Its straight-gripped stock and splinter forend are built so that the pattern is placed high—say a half-pattern above the point of aim at thirty yards. The balance is to the rear so the gun is distinctly muzzle light for faster handling and faster point.

"Butt, Belly, Beak, *Bang*"

Now comes the pointing part. I'm not the best shot in the world, and what I know of woodcock shooting comes from several decades of missing them in every way known to either me *or* the woodcock. The woodcock rarely presents chances for a long lead or even a smooth mount, overtake, and follow-through. As I said earlier, woodcock shooting is a look-and-stab proposition most days in most places.

Of the methods of wing shooting, the so-called "modified snap" shot is the one the good shooters most often employ, and so it should be the one the rest of us lousy shots copy. In this method the bird is first seen and seen clearly. A rapid judgment is made of its angle of flight and probable path of escape, which with woodcock is usually through the opening in the canopy of leaves overhead.

The gun is mounted while the swing is taking place, the shooter's body pivoting at the waist to overtake the bird. The start from behind, catch, and get-ahead movements are all being executed before the gun is fully mounted so that when it is, you are swinging with the bird and you are already accurately ahead of it when lead is required.

When the butt is settled in your shoulder pocket, the correct lead has been achieved. It is essential to shoot before the swing has come to a stop: the *instant* the butt is settled in. The British often teach a method whereby the trigger finger has pressure on the trigger so that the force of the butt coming back against the shoulder causes the hand to slide back minutely and the trigger to be pulled. It works. That's how fast the shot should come. The swing, the lead—these are established while the gun is still coming up. On a bird that is crossing at a slight angle, the gun should come to your face ahead of the bird and in motion along the bird's path of flight. Don't hesitate. In fact, the British have a little saying for this drill that makes sense and points out the need for catching the bird, swinging through, and firing. It goes: "Butt, belly, beak, *bang.*"

Since most shooting comes over a dog that is on point rather than flushing, you can greatly increase your luck by watching the dog and looking things over. Usually with woodcock a solid point gives you a chance to plan things out a bit. Take a minute to look at the surrounding cover. Look for holes of daylight in the overhead canopy. It is to these holes that the woodcock is likely—likely, mind you—to head once flushed. Position yourself so that you are more or less facing this hole. Then you'll get a high incidence of straightaway shots.

In fairly open cover 'cock go out lower and faster, usually staying at eye level and zig-zagging a lot; in thick cover they normally jump straight up. If your dog points in thick stuff or is holding a bird well in fairly open cover, approaching the dog head-on will cause the bird to come straight up most of the time. Shoot when he tops out. In many cases knowing what the bird is likely to do when flushed helps your shooting—it has mine.

Woodcock are missed with regularity by some pretty good shots. They are not easy targets because of their habit of living where it's tough to get gun to shoulder some days. And like all eye-hand activities, wing shooting offers the chance for slumps, the seemingly unexplainable times when we are doing what we have always done and nothing seems to work.

But the reason for slumps is, essentially, that we are doing something wrong, something mechanical that once corrected lets us return to our normal, legendary form.

Let's assume that you haven't been up all night drinking Scotch whiskey, that you are more or less well coordinated, and that you have the proper frame of mind—concentration on the task at hand. Let's say that the birds are in their normal coverts and the shots are of the normal sort for woodcock: short range, ahead of a good dog. After that, of course, there are few "normal" shots at woodcock. If we agree on these factors, then, let's go ahead and look at some misses and some reasons.

Too Slow

Some days woodcock seem to fly faster than other days. On overcast days they see better and fly better; the reverse is true on bright days. But when they all seem to be flying too fast, there could be reasons why we are just too slow.

One reason could be that the balance of the gun is not right. A good woodcock gun should balance behind the hinge pin. A gun with its weight farther forward seems to move slower, and indeed it does. Some days even a light gun with its balance at the right spot is too slow.

Also, as we age our intensity, our need to bag birds, diminishes, and this manifests itself in a bit of slowness. And with older shooters, hearing, the first sense a woodcock hunter uses, becomes less acute and so we aren't aware of the birds until they are well up.

On days when you're feeling sluggish or your age, I would recommend a very light gun, which is against my better judgment otherwise. For example, I have shot wood-cock with a sixteen-gauge for years. It is under six pounds—a lightweight. Still, some days even this feels too heavy. It is then that I go to an ultralight twenty-eight gauge, a little sidelock with twenty-five-inch barrels that weighs five pounds even. I wish the barrels were longer—say twenty-seven and a half inches, but the gun was not available in that gauge with that barrel length, so I took potluck. This gun is the fastest I have ever shot at woodcock. Not the most effec-tive, mind you, but the fastest. In fact, the quickness is its undoing because another whole host of problems comes with shooting *too* fast. But on days when I somehow feel slow, the twenty-eight tunes me up.

As you grow older and the hillsides become steeper, you may want to trade a twelve for a twenty, or a twelve for a sixteen, or a sixteen for a twenty, or even a twenty for a twenty-eight. All of these guns are ballistically fine for wood-cock, a fragile bird shot at the closest ranges of any of the upland birds. Remember: Twenty yards is a long shot in woodcock cover, and at that range a three-fourth ounce of shot from a twenty-eight or an ounce from a twelve are moot points to the bird.

Instead of changing guns, you can speed up points by changing the hold your barrel hand has on the forend, or barrels. A shorter hold will allow you to more quickly move the barrels compared with a longer hold, which smooths things out by slowing things down. Try it in your own home by snapping off some dry points with the gun held with a shorter hold. I think you'll be surprised at the way the gun comes up faster.

Wrong Choke

Sometimes the choke in the gun is wrong. At close range any choke is often too much. I went over the statistics I keep on woodcock shot, and the last seventy birds were hit at the following ranges: sixty-one birds at twenty-one yards or under; nine at twenty-two yards or over. I picked twenty-one yards because that is the range that skeet chokes (about cylinder) are bored to give their optimum pattern spread and density, and at that range there is virtually no difference in killing efficiency among the gauges (the .410 aside).

So if you are shooting the traditional improved cylinder/ modified often called for in a woodcock gun, you may want to have the right barrel opened up to straight cylinder or skeet, especially if the hits you are making seem to shred birds.

Patterning your gun at the ranges in which you are actually hitting birds does far more than computing percentages from skeets shot at forty yards. Here is a chart that gives some of the pattern spreads accepted at various ranges from various chokes.

Pattern Spread in Inches

			range in yards				
choke	*10*	*15*	*20*	*25*	*30*	*35*	*40*
True cylinder	20″	26″	32″	38″	44″	51″	58″
Improved cylinder	15	20	26	32	38	44	51
Modified	12	16	21	26	32	38	45
Full	9	12	16	21	27	33	40

As you can see from this chart, it is approximately twice as easy to hit a bird with a cylinder pattern at fifteen yards compared with a full-choke pattern, and a modified barrel does not come into its own until the ranges are somewhere around twenty-five yards. In many cases that is much farther than you will even have a chance at woodcock, especially in the early season before the birds have flighted and before the cover has dropped.

Head Lifting

When a woodcock flushes, he is often hard to see because of brush and cover. Even when we can see him, the excitement may make us lift our heads to get a better view of what's going on: The gun barrels rise with the rising eye, and we miss by shooting over. Even the bill of a baseball cap pulled low over the eyes gets in the way, making us lift our heads to see under it.

A straight-gripped gun helps keep the face down by driving it onto the stock because of the angle the triggering hand must take to properly hold the gun. But most head lifting can be corrected by concentration, making yourself consciously feel the pressure of the stock on your face.

As a shooter gains experience, he very often takes a stock with less drop than he used to need. A straight stock with little drop allows you to shoot up at a bird, thus eliminating the need for head lifting. If your old gun is starting to miss, maybe it's time for a new fitting to see if you've changed.

Conversely, as we age we often need more drop than we used to because of our stiffening joints and tightening muscles. Then the reverse is the answer—we need a gun with more drop, a much easier job for a good gunsmith to accomplish than raising the comb.

Wrong Foot Position

Good woodcock shots are good shots because, no matter what the cover is like, they never seem to be out of position; they always seem to be able to get off a well-pointed, well-timed shot. The main reason for this success is foot position; good shots rarely have both feet off the ground at the same time. By this I mean they have learned little tricks that enable them to get into action at any time.

One such trick is that they always take an obstacle—a downed tree or limb, a puddle, a rock—by stepping over it left foot first (for right-handers). Since the normal shooting position for a right-handed shooter is with the left foot slightly ahead of the right, this means that they always hit the ground nearly in shooting position.

Likewise, when a patch of brush proves especially thick and the good shot finds he has to bull his way through it, he does so with his left shoulder first, his gun and his right, or shooting, side protected and ready for action. After a while such actions become automatic, and in the course of a season they allow for hits when there would otherwise be misses.

Stabbing

Stabbing is the act of snatching at the bird: lifting the head, stopping the swing (what there is of it), and spot shooting. The shooter's teeth are gritted, his eyes bugged out. You know the shot—the desperate, ultrafast one that rarely hits.

One of the reasons for snatching is, sadly, competition with another shooter, trying to be first to take a bird, to be slicker than the other guy. Many times a stretch at hunting alone corrects this and reintroduces well-timed shooting habits.

The main way to break the habit, though, is to concentrate on seeing the bird clearly before you even mount the gun. Consciously think of the shot as a one-two-three proposition: viewing the bird, raising the gun, taking the shot. Say the words out loud as you go through the drill; it smooths everything out nicely. You may even want to try the British "butt, belly, beak, *bang*" method. And as far as competition goes, get it straight with fellow hunters that woodcock hunting to you isn't like tennis or golf; there are no scores kept.

What I've said about slow shooting aside, most of us have more time than we think to trigger a shot. A difference of a few feet or a couple of yards only helps your pattern spread and increases your odds of hitting. The superb shot shoots only as fast as he has to; when you are really on and a woodcock flushes and flies across a little opening, you will be dropping the bird just as it hits the far edge of the cover, a split second before it would be gone. Then you are using every bit of range and pattern spread to your advantage.

Waiting for a Better Shot

Sometimes you can wait a whole season. If you wait for a bird to clear cover, you won't get birds. Very few woodcock are shot except through cover. Even a light load of fine shot can search and kill in thick cover, so shoot. Shoot as if the trees and the brush and the limbs were not there. If you wait for a 'cock to come out the other side, most of the time he won't. You must shoot when you are ready; otherwise swing and trigger timing are all messed up.

One of the finest ways to sharpen your shooting skills for woodcock, and for many other birds, is through sporting clays, a game that by now has become quite well known in this country.

Sporting clays is using clay targets to simulate the flight of specific gamebird species in more or less natural conditions. The game originated in England, where it is now the single most popular shooting sport. On this continent the number of courses offering quality shooting is increasing yearly.

Interestingly, bird hunters seem to be gravitating toward the sport, for good reason. The targets are released from hidden traps, the flights are never exactly the same, and there is a delay between the call to pull and the release of the target.

But the best part is that sporting clays does not allow the shooter to even mount the gun until the target is in clear view. Thus the entire wing-shooting drill is called for. You must see the bird, mount the gun, establish lead, shoot, and follow through. At most stations doubles are the rule, so there is no time to dwell on the target.

In other clay-target shooting, methodical perfection has become the rule. In trap and skeet, 100 and 200 straights are the rule in big tournaments. But in sporting clays this isn't true. There has never been a perfect score shot at sporting clays in a tournament in this country, and 85 x 100 will put you among the best in the world at this game.

Since there is such a premium on gun handling, most serious competitors shoot doubles (mostly over–unders), but some (including Your Favorite Woodcock Hunter) shoot side by sides.

If you know of a sporting-clays course near you, give it a try. It is a fun game unto itself and is the best practice there is for what clay target shooting is supposed to be: bird shooting.

4

Woodcock Dogs

With the possible exception of sage grouse hunting, there is no wing-shooting sport where a dog adds so much as woodcock hunting. Sage grouse, in the wayback where they are lightly hunted, actually need a dog to make them more sporty. Hunters they know nothing of, and so they are likely to come up to look you over; a dog that approximates a coyote makes them a better adversary.

And with the exception of quail hunting in the old Grand Manner, there is no shooting sport where the animal adds so much in terms of style and grace—and efficiency—as woodcock hunting.

Woodcock were created for a pointing dog because even a rather crude one can do a good job on woodcock, and an average dog looks like Who Finished First At Grand Junction handling these birds. The woodcock's scent must be strong for its size, and the scent must lie well, because dogs that have never encountered them before usually become avid pointers of the bird after just a few meetings. Further, the woodcock do not run that much, and here let me tell you a story that will disprove some of the things you may have read about woodcock running.

Running Birds

There are those who say that a woodcock will not run ahead of a dog, that they are ungainly and they waddle and so they sit tight and depend on concealment and camouflage for protection. These same folks claim that when the dog points, breaks, relocates and points again several yards ahead, he is first following a preexisting scent trail and then finding the location of the bird that just made the scent trail. These theories are always interesting to me because they are usually born of rationalization about why a dog with a pedigree as long as your leg can't, on occasion, hold a li'l ol' woodcock. People will come up with strange things to protect the integrity of their dogs, whether that integrity is real or imagined.

The theory, friend, is wrong. Woodcock *do* run—if you can call it that. Actually, they sort of scurry along under cover of ferns or low-hanging brush across open forest floor. Many times they will break into a short two- or three-wingbeat flight, thus doing a good job of breaking the scent trail slightly. Last season I saw this act on eight occasions—four in one day.

My dog was having a tough time with the birds in the covert my son and I were hunting. She would point, break, relocate, and then point again, much in the way that she tries to handle running grouse. Eventually, many yards from where she started, she would again point the bird, usually in thick ground cover. Finally, I got down on my hands and knees and watched what was going on. Here came a woodcock, looking like a wind-up tin soldier, with my dog snuffling along behind. When the bird took the short flight I mentioned earlier, the dog got confused until she reestab-

Author's setter pup, Jess, is being trained to whoa (author uses "steady" to avoid confusion with "no"). A young dog should always be on a check cord until you are sure of control. Notice that the dog is also wearing her bell during training to get used to listening to her owner's voice over the sound of the bell.

lished the scent trail. Chris saw several birds do the same thing.

My pal Don Chilcote, regional representative of the Ruffed Grouse Society, says that flight birds do this more often than immediately flushing, perhaps because they are tired or maybe because they are reluctant to leave cover in a strange area without knowing where they're going next. I agree with Don because on every occasion that I've observed this behavior, it's been during an identifiable flight. The day I saw all those running birds, we had forty-four woodcock flushes in two hours in a cover that three days earlier had held two birds.

So, woodcock do run and will run, and flight birds are more likely to run than birds that are natives and haven't begun migrating.

As a result, the woodcock dog will encounter running birds. I don't mean to have a coronary over a few woodcock ambling ahead of a dog; they aren't in the rooster–pheasant class of sprinters, and they don't run very far. But many times they will run to a point at which their flush cuts off any chance of a shot—a pretty slick way of doing things on their part.

Picking a Pointer

Now, to the dogs. Among the pointing class of dogs, virtually any pointing breed can do a good job on woodcock. It seems that the earlier a dog is introduced to the birds the better, but I've seen some older dogs, trained on other birds, that took to woodcock quite naturally. One of these was a crackerjack quail dog, a singles specialist, that a friend brought north for the early-season gunning one year. A little pointer, she was one of those thorough busybodies that search out every bit of cover, and she found a fair number of birds. She was a bit confused at first, though my friend told me that she pointed a few woodcock every year in the South while hunting quail, so she wasn't totally unaccustomed to them. But she *was* unaccustomed to having the guns go off

An old campaigner with a woodcock nailed. Woodcock were absolutely made for a pointing dog because they lie so well, depending upon their camouflage for protection.

when she pointed a 'cock. Apparently my pal and his friends didn't shoot woodcock when they hunted quail. Don't ask me why not because I didn't ask him. I was just grateful.

The range of a pointing dog for woodcock is one of some speculation. Almost universally, men who know dogs like close work for these birds, mostly because wider ranging puts the dog out of sight. But there are those who, confident their dogs can hold a bird on point, don't mind if the dog is out of sight. The trick then is keeping track of where the dog is so you can hunt him up when the bell stops.

Color is important. I think one thing the fine Gordon setter has going against it is its black-and-tan coloration, making the dog tough to see in the coverts. Blaze orange collars don't help all that much, and even the blaze orange vests you can buy for dogs are a nuisance. A white or predominantly white dog is the best choice, and a variety of breeds are of this color: English setters, pointers, Brittanies, even some of the continental versatile breeds like the wirehair and the griffon, have enough white on them to be seen easily.

For visibility's sake a pair of dogs, trained to back or honor point, are the best. That way at least one of the dogs is visible in cover. Many times it is the honoring dog that points the way to the dog with the bird under his nose.

Coloration sometimes affects the perception of range. My setter is an orange belton, ticked with orange on white. At fifteen yards she doesn't show any of the orange, only the white. I can see her at quite a distance, even in thick cover; a darker dog would be thought to be ranging too far even if he were not one step farther out than Jess. Jim Nelson's Irish setter, Big Al, was a top-drawer 'cock dog despite his autumn red color.

Obviously, the woodcock dog should be staunch on point. The bird offers so many chances for points that style on point can be readily addressed. A dog that points with head high, a nose full of rising scent, tail erect, is a sight. The tail is a flag that shows where the rest of the dog is, including the part that smelled the bird. A long, high tail is not just an

A woodcock dog should be, in most hunters' opinions, predominantly white. Here the setter stands out in the thick brush when on point. Note the shooter in the background moving in to flush.

The happy little English springer spaniel makes a fine woodcock dog for those who like the flushing breeds. However, as with all flushers, it is essential that the dog be within range—within sight—or his work will be for nothing. A flushing dog rousts birds into the air for the gun, but if he is ranging too wide and too far out, there will be no shooter available when he puts birds up.

affectation on a woodcock dog, it actually does some good. The docked-tailed dogs (Britts, griffons) don't have this little extra, but they make up for it with drive.

I have hunted woodcock with all of the breeds that point birds. There are bad ones in all breeds. I have never been a breed snob. I admire a dog that does well whatever it is he is bred and trained to do, and I like to think that most good dogs have a certain personality typical of good dogs, not necessarily typical of the breed.

For example, most good woodcock dogs are what you might call a little "soft." They are less slash and fire, more snoop here and snoop there, not pottering, just thorough. They are usually friendly to a fault—which doesn't have any impact on their hunting at all, it's just an observation—and they are usually devoted to one man. They hunt for that man and for themselves. Woodcock hunting seems to be a personal experience, much more personal than big-country quail hunting, where fresh dogs are released in braces to cruise the timbered sedge fields. Woodcock and their coverts are intimate entities, and this intimacy is carried over into the relationship between man and dog.

Good woodcock dogs, like all good dogs, also seem to be exceptionally smart. This may be a matter of intelligence or of spending so much time with just one person. The dog comes to read the person, and therefore his intelligence level seems to rise. Most woodcock hunters I know live with their dogs inside and all year. This closeness pays off in the autumn, when the unspoken teamwork is important.

The traits I've described are present in all the breeds. Show me a man who says: "This or that breed is no good for woodcock," and I'll show you a man who hasn't hunted behind many dogs. When you say stuff like that, you're branding yourself a beginner.

Training

The woodcock dog should cover his ground thoroughly and should do it at a merry pace, not ranging so far as to get

Author's setter, Jess, with the product of a morning's hunt—two woodcock and a grouse. Where the birds intermingle, an experienced dog learns to handle each species differently, being more bold on woodcock because of their propensity to hold, and being more cautious on grouse. However, a dog with a lot of fire and slash is likely to hold grouse well, too, seemingly dumbfounding the birds until the hunter gets there. Woodcock, to the pointing-dog man, are a blessing because they'll make an average dog look like a crackerjack.

lost when the bell stops, but also not licking your boots. He should quarter the cover as much as the cover will allow. Some smart old campaigners sort of sashay their way through the cover, nose up in the breeze, and then head off when they hit scent, a very efficient manner for dogs who still have the odd half day left in them a couple of times a week. One twelve-year-old setter bitch I knew hunted this way, following deer trails at a slow trot until she hit bird scent and then angling off for the point. She missed some birds, but she pointed a lot of them she didn't miss. It didn't take long for me to figure out there was no future in popping brush, so I followed her on the deer trails. When her tail went up and she headed off the trail, I was right with her. After a hunt like that, I wasn't even winded and neither was she. I guess that's how you get to be a twelve-year-old setter.

A dog should be trained to obey hand signals. Many times, from your vantage point, you can see cover you'd like the dog to look over. The hand signals allow you to direct the dog this way or thataway and keep talking to a minimum in the woods. I think talking affects woodcock less than, say, grouse, but a lot of talk will still make them less likely to hold well for a classy point, and they seem to be tougher shots when they do go up—maybe they're already excited from their fear of the voices. Perhaps "alarm" is better than "fear," but you get the idea.

Pointing dogs should be equipped with bells so you can tell there is a point when the bell becomes silent. These are merry little sounds, but many shooters are going to beepers, which give off a *beep* when the dog stops on point, allowing you to locate him better. I guess they are a clever idea, and they are quite popular, but I don't like them. Seems like the dog is a robot out there, and it takes some of the fun out of things, like trying to find a dog on point because you were daydreaming and don't remember where he was last. Still, if I hunted with dark-colored dogs, I'd probably use a beeper. In heavy brush you can look right at a staunch Gordon and not see him.

Flushing dogs have their place in the woodcock thickets,

In thick brush, the modern version of the bell is this electronic beeper, which gives off a regular cadence when the dog stops and is on point.

oddly enough. There are fine Labs and springer spaniels that have been trained on these birds and do a good job of rooting them into the air. The English cocker spaniel—a pint-sized springer in looks and style—was originally developed as a woodcock dog, the "cocker" being a cannibalization of the word "woodcocker." My pal Jack Morris has a little cocker I've hunted behind, and this dog leaves no scrap of cover uninvestigated. The dog's color is predominantly white, so he's easy to see. His range is very close, necessary for any flushing dog in cover.

Another friend I have hunted with insists on using a springer that is rarely, if ever, in control or in range. This animal busts birds out of range, which is to say out of sight. The important thing to remember is that if the dog is there to flush birds for your gun, the flushing must take place where you have a chance for a shot. If not, then the dog is no good until properly trained.

But all talk of flushing dogs aside, the real woodcock hunter—not the person who hunts them incidentally to other game—is better off with a pointing dog. The Brittany is a popular dog, but I lean toward dogs with long tails. I've had English pointers, and the best woodcock dog I ever saw was a pointer, but most are too hot for me to handle well. So I've settled on setters because of their style, looks, and personality. But, boy, I love any dog that does his job well, and I'll happily hunt behind your *Whattsithund* if the beast can point woodcock well.

Hire a Professional?

The busy woodcock hunter, one without the time to train his own dog, might consider the use of a professional trainer. But there are some warnings I'd like to give you before you do this. First, there is the question of finances. A gun dog is a big investment these days and represents a whole economy involving puppies, finished dogs, training aids and so forth. This economy is a big one and getting bigger as more and more people own and use dogs for sport. Thus there will always be those who deliver less than they promise. Many of them quickly revert to whatever they did before becoming full-time dog trainers, but there are still some out there.

Let's say that a trainer wants to charge you $200 a month for training your dog, and he says the dog will be worked on woodcock (or grouse). To do an economically feasible job, the trainer will usually have twenty dogs in for training at any one time. Now if he works twelve hours a day, seven days a week (and many of them do), this means your dog will get a little over four hours a week of training, or sixteen hours for the month. For the trainer that figures out to a little over twelve dollars an hour, not very good wages for any professional these days, but most trainers love the life and its rewards.

Will all of this work be on woodcock? I'm afraid not. I'm sure it will be in woodcock *cover*, but I'm just as sure that the bird work will be on the ubiquitous planted pigeon, not on woodcock, because there are simply not enough woodcock anywhere to keep twenty dogs busy seven days a week, twelve hours a day. The advice, then, is to accept the training if you must under the conditions that exist, but don't pay a long dollar because your dog will be worked on woodcock only; he won't.

Scents and Sensibility

How you go about using the dog in cover can make a difference in how well the two of you do. I think the most effective hunting combination is two shooters and one dog. One man and one dog are often left silent and shotless because the birds come up behind cover, where you have no shot. With two people, one walking in on point and the other watching another likely escape route, you'll do better.

The wind is rarely a problem in the sheltered coverts, but it normally exists to some degree in autumn, and you have to consider it. Working a dog with his back to the wind negates some of the power of that great nose, and it makes for wild flushes and bumped birds much more readily than working the dog and the cover into the wind. Oddly enough, some dogs have a nose that is almost *too* good. My setter is this way, and some days when the scenting is exceptional, she almost drives me to drink (a very short drive) because she'll point many yards from the bird. By the time I find the bird, the dog is usually out of sight behind me, giving me no help at all in pinpointing location. But that same great nose has enabled her to nail birds for me that were several yards downwind from her. It took me a while to understand that she could wind a bird downwind that far, so I missed chances. Now I believe her.

A dog with a great nose, aided by the wind, is able to cover his ground faster and with more confidence, although it does not always work out that way. There are dogs with great noses that still tippy-toe around, afraid they've missed something. My own dog does this once in a while, usually after a great shoot in which there were birds under nearly every alder. If there are few woodcock the next trip out, she sometimes does a little—frankly—false pointing at the odd splashing. Makes me mad as hell, but the other side is that we don't ever bump or walk past a bird.

When the dog is on point, it is your responsibility to get there quickly. Doing so keeps the bird pretty well frozen in place and it keeps your dog intense. A few words to the dog to reassure him help, and then you walk in. Walk in from the side—ninety degrees to the dog's line of point. This way the dog can see you and won't get excited and also won't have to stand there with shotguns going off right over his head. If the bird is in very thick cover and there is a chance for it, try approaching the dog from the front. The bird, pinched between you and the dog, will normally rise straight up, the easiest of all woodcock shots provided you are standing under the bird.

And watch the cover overhead. Woodcock will head for openings in the canopy of leaves, and if you are positioned so that you can flush the bird and keep an opening covered, you'll have a leg up in getting a good shot.

Dogs have a use in woodcock banding, but let me tell you

Author moves in to flush a bird pointed in a neck of alders stretching into a field. Note that he is coming in from the side, which shows the dog where he is and also cuts down the bird's possible escape angles. From the approach, the bird will probably come up in the small opening between the two clumps of alders directly ahead of the dog.

that if you want to band birds, a tried performer is the only dog to consider, not an eager pup or a dog being trained. Banding is an important function of woodcock management, way too important to have a heavy-footed, uncouth mutt start stomping and gulping baby woodcock.

Retrieving the Game

My dog is not a finished woodcock dog because she will not retrieve downed birds. She'll find them for me, usually by flash pointing them with a quick twist of her head, but you'd better be looking, brother, because she won't go back and show you again unless you make a Federal Case out of it.

There is a lot said about dogs not fetching woodcock, but I have seen more that will than ones that won't. No dog is ever really finished unless it retrieves because the loss of game due to crippling is a loss that can be prevented, unlike losses to the weather and predation. My dog will fetch grouse, quail, pheasants, and so forth, but woodcock are beyond her.

Normally, Labs and springers are the best retrievers of woodcock because they don't seem to mind the bird's loose feathers, or whatever it is that makes some dogs refuse to mouth and handle the dead thing that only moments before they had pursued so diligently.

So if you, like me, have stopped trying to get your dog to fetch, you must be your own woodcock finder. The first thing you must do is convince yourself that the bird is there after it's down. With flighting woodcock under every alder, it is hard to stop the whole hunt to find one downed bird, but to do less is unsportsmanlike at the very least. The second thing is to realize that woodcock are very civilized about waiting right about where they dropped; crippled runners are unheard of except in rare cases. I've only seen a few, and they were very lightly hit.

Actually, the hardest bird for me to find is the one that drops stone dead almost in the open. The bird is air washed and now, in death, is not giving off fresh scent. I have seen dogs that were excellent retrievers kick birds with their paws accidentally, this motion stirring up enough scent to enable them to home in; other times the bird is virtually invisible, especially if it drops on a background of dead oak leaves—the worst.

If two shooters see a bird go down, it is best for one of them to stay put, eyes glued to the spot where he last saw the form. The other hunter, usually the shooter, likewise keeps his eyes on a mark (a stick, a leaf, a tuft of grass) and heads straight toward it. Through triangulation the bird's location is pretty well pinned down. If the 'cock is not right there, place your hat on the ground immediately, right in the area you expected to find the bird, and start making circles around the hat, wider all the time, scuffing your feet. Try to get your dog to help; there may be some residual scent or you may stir some up yourself. This system will usually do it. Once I couldn't see the bird and so I tossed my hat down and started circling. Finally, I gave up and went to retrieve my hat. As you probably figured out by now, the bird was under the hat. Another time Chris shot three woodcock in succession during a flight, and he saw not one of them fall—but I did from a different vantage point and found them for him.

Training the Pup

A woodcock dog's training, like that of any dog used to point birds, should start with his selection as a pup. Since there are thirty times more ways to select a pup than there are ways to select a spouse, let's dispense with that part of it. Suffice it to say that perhaps the very aggressive puppy should be left for the man who is looking for a pheasant dog.

The pup should be removed from the litter at six or seven weeks of age for greater socialization with his human companion. Psychologically, we don't want the dog to really understand he is a dog; his life is to be spent with humans in the very human pursuit of woodcock hunting, so the faster the dog gets with humans the better, once he is weaned from his mother.

I say "he" a lot here, but frankly I think that females make better woodcock dogs. At least most of the good ones I have seen have been females because they seem to be much more fastidious in working cover; males generally exhibit more fire. But there are real smokers in either sex. A female seems to me to want to please more, and—although I sure can't prove it and even hesitate to mention it—female hunting dogs seem to be closer to men than male dogs, which seem to gravitate more to women.

The pup should learn that you are the greatest thing in the world. Take him with you in the car so that he gets used to riding; talk to him and pet him and praise him. A well-controlled dog is one that wants to please, not one that fears to do wrong.

The dog should have the basics of training instilled at an early age, the meaning of "come," "sit," "stay," and so forth. Since I use the term "no" when I want the dog to stop whatever he's doing, I don't use "whoa" to freeze the dog when he is close to a bird and I fear he's going to bump it. The two words sound too much alike; I use "steady" instead of "whoa." Whatever you use, the dog has to be taught the meaning of it. This is best done with a good training book and a lot of repetition, working with the pup until his attention lags or you feel your temper start to rise like a thing alive. Then quit for the day.

Another word about professional trainers. Many good woodcock dogs are soft, and many fine trainers are hard because their methods are developed with speed in mind. This discrepancy can be a problem if your dog is not as aggressive as some others. The electronic training collar is a godsend for some trainers, but others misuse it for something other than fault correction, and this practice can drive an introspective dog even further into his shell. Now no one wants a timid dog, but some dogs respond more to the one-on-one training only the owner can give him. These dogs, once trained, make the best hunters and are the most satisfying to hunt with because we've trained them ourselves—or they've trained us.

If you can't live without it, you can put a woodcock wing on a string to test the dog's pointing instincts, but doing so is a parlor trick rather than real training, and a little bit of it goes a long way. You are better off concentrating on getting the dog in front of you and exploring cover. At first, walking the dog around your yard and having him poke into the shrubbery is fine; later, move to an open field, and finally into woodcock-type cover. Once you have started to work the dog in this type of cover, never work him in the open again unless you are correcting faults. His life is in the brush.

While training, never let the dog off a check cord—the plastic clothesline kind slips easily through cover. I have a friend whose setter is a real coyote; she's never seen a check cord. You must imprint the dog's mind with the knowledge that you can reach him and stop him anytime you want, and that's just what a check cord does.

Hand signals are valuable for woodcock dogs because they keep talking to a minimum. With a wave of the hand you can send the dog to a piece of cover you want him to check out. Signaling is best taught early in the open by waving your hand in an exaggerated throwing motion and walking in the direction of the "throw." The dog will scurry over to get ahead of you. Then do it again in another direction. Soon he will head for your intended area with only the wave of your hand. My dog and I do this often, and it's like free beer on days when she has more energy than I do, which is almost always.

The dog should also be taught to hunt dead, at least help you find downed woodcock, even if he won't pick them up. One way of teaching him is to scatter pieces of weenie or doggie treats in the grass and tell him to "hunt dead" while you are making a palm-down circular motion over the area you want him to search, the palm of your hand parallel to the ground. Once he starts finding treats where you indicate, he will be very eager to look whenever you ask him to.

The only thing left is to work the dog—in good cover and as often as possible. Bird contact is the only thing that will make a woodcock dog, and the more the better.

5

Impedimenta

The gear of woodcock hunting, the things we gather about us, falls into a couple of categories. First, there are the necessities, the things we really need: guns, dogs, clothing, vehicles, and so forth. Without these things we would not hunt or we would hunt in a manner that would make us less than the effective sort we are.

The other category is the gear we like, want, and may or may not use, and the stuff that smacks of the tradition in which our sport is steeped.

Dressing for Comfort

The experienced brush hunter, be he after woodcock, ruffed grouse, or wayward bobwhites who don't know they belong in sedge fields, probably already knows a lot of the following information, but it bears repeating. First, most woodcock hunting is done throughout the bird's range in near-summer conditions and temperatures. The opening day this year in my home state was exceptionally warm—over seventy-five degrees—and it stayed that way for a week. Even a long-sleeved shirt seemed like a hardship in that weather. The bugs and the sweat and the warm wind all made hunting seem nothing like what you see on the fall catalogs or calendars. It was tough.

Thus we have to understand that to be effective, to make the most of the days we have in the woods, and—this is important—to *enjoy ourselves*, we have to be dressed right for the task at hand. An overheated woodcock hunter is one having no fun and asking for trouble.

I used to be big on brush pants, the kind with the nylon facing that turns briars (ha!). Not any more. Instead, I wear a light pair of khaki cotton pants that I get from outdoor catalog houses for about twenty bucks a pop. They do not turn briars—not by a long shot—but they are cool. I turn the thorns by wearing knee-high rubber boots, the kind sold by importers dealing in British shooting accouterments. These come to the knees, and that's where most of the briar damage is anyway, so I'm not miserable in thick cover, and the cotton breathes, unlike nylon.

Besides protecting my lower legs, the boots have decent support and are waterproof, naturally. They are called Wellies and are sold by a number of firms and catalogers. You tuck the pant legs inside, and even in the rain you'll have dry feet if your socks are snug enough. Additionally, in wet weather the pants sticking out the top tend to collect water and whisk it away from my legs, keeping me drier than my pals in briar pants and leather boots, all of which leak no matter what anyone says about them.

The best boots, though, for most people are the ones with the rubber bottoms and leather tops (the kind sold by L.L. Bean, for instance); second would be all-leather with good support, although all-leather boots will eventually leak like the State Department, and in wet cover—where woodcock are found—leaks can get uncomfortable.

This young shooter, author's son Jason, with a woodcock he bagged while wearing the accepted uniform of the day: brush pants, a light shell vest with pin-on compass, and a blaze orange hat. As a young shooter, his twenty-gauge double is perfect for him. Many beginners are mistakenly given a .410 because it has a lighter recoil; however, the .410 can be a crippler and is an expert's gun. Very few people are capable of using it on woodcock. Instead, the twenty has little recoil when shot with light loads and makes the beginning hunter more effective.

For a shirt, light cotton is nice. I wear a white shirt because my dog, being colorblind, can see me better when I'm waving my arms at her. There are a number of nice-looking and nice-fitting shirts around; just be sure you get one that won't bind you during gun mounting.

Vest Essentials

The vest is a traveling pack of supplies. It is intended to hold the few shells we'll fire and the fewer birds we'll bag between trips to the car. It can also be used to carry a number of other things, all of which can make the day a little more delightful (or less disastrous).

One of these things is a dog first-aid kit. I have carried one for years, have had to use it a couple of times, and wouldn't be without it. It weighs about as much as a half box of sixteen-gauge shells, but it could save my dog's life someday. You can buy such a kit commercially, or you can have your vet make one up for you. The commercial ones have instruction books that can help you with injuries and treatment in case you slept through the canine health course in veterinary school. A number of things can happen to a dog afield, and a hard-working dog takes a beating when hunting more than a couple of times a week or several days in a row. Most of these injuries are superficial, but some can be bad. Never put your dog in the car for the ride home without checking him thoroughly—the results of such an oversight can be disastrous.

These kits should contain topical painkillers, eye dope, antiseptic, smelling salts, elastic bandage materials, adhesive tape, quick-freeze packs (plastic packs that get very cold when the contents are squeezed and mixed together through the plastic), hemostats, large-gauge pads, and anything else you can think of.

If you, like I, are prone to wandering off to where no man has ever gone before, you should also carry a compass. About once a year, sometimes more, I get pretty lost. I have a hard time with moss on the sides of trees and finding the

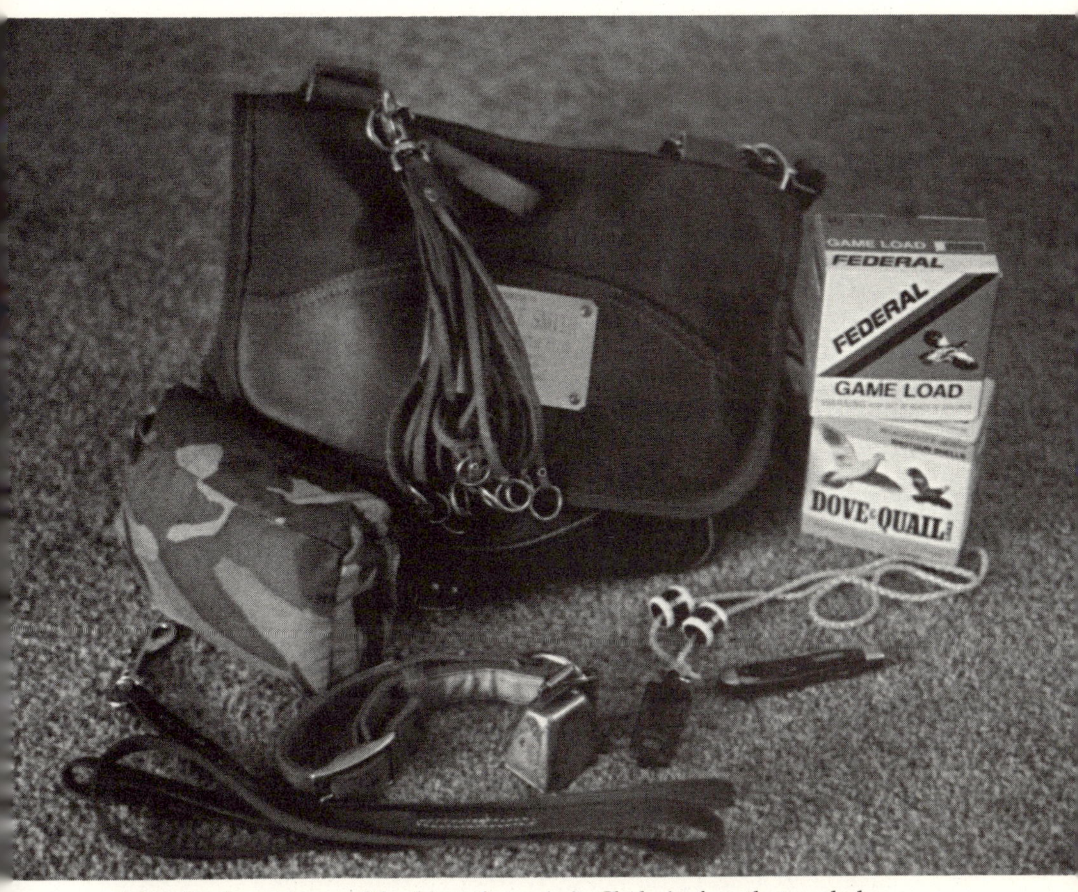

A shoulder bag and some of the things that go in it. Clockwise from the top: the bag with bird loops for holding the birds, shot shells, a dog whistle and flush counters on a lanyard, a pocketknife, a blaze orange collar with a bell, a dog lead, and a self-contained first-aid kit for dogs.

direction from the setting sun because usually at sunset I like to be parked somewhere behind a sundowner. So I wear a compass and I use it—most of the time. To use a compass properly, you have to look at the thing to know what direction you headed into a covert. If, for example, you headed east away from the car, then you will eventually have to head west to find the car again, unless you want to walk around the world and come in the back way.

Compasses are also great when you're hunting with a companion, as in: "Let's head north for a half mile or so and then we'll turn west." If you are both carrying compasses, there won't be a discussion about which way those directions are unless you read your compass next to your gun barrel, in which case the gun barrel will always be north. The pin-on kind are almost a requirement of brush hunters, the little orbital balls being the best. Pessimists get the kind with directions that glow in the dark.

I also like to load the vest up with goodies, like doggie treats and candy and things (candy for me). A little pint canteen of water is nice in dry country, where your dog might need a drink, but usually woodcock cover has water nearby, and a pint *is* a pound the world around unless it's in your shooting vest, in which case it's a ton.

The vest itself should be fairly light because of the weather and all the stuff you'll stuff into it. The blaze orange kind is hard to beat. Remington makes my current favorite. I glow like a neon sign for others to see, especially those others with shotguns. I have a prairie type for very warm weather, which is nothing more than several pockets suspended with straps. A leather tie keeps the brush from pulling the straps off my shoulders.

More Gear

The hat isn't a hat unless it shades your eyes, keeps the rain off you, stays on in thick cover, and protects your graying, thinning locks. The baseball-cap style does almost none of these; the little tweed jobs the yuppies wear to work at the stock brokerage do. Get one and try it. Additionally, the smaller brim means you won't pick up your head during gun mounting to see out from under a big hat brim, so your face stays down on the stock better.

Shooting gloves allow you to keep from bleeding to death from thorn scratches and also to keep a grip on the gun if you get sweaty, but early in the season they are a bother because they get warm. Try a light glove, maybe a golf glove, on whichever hand you prefer. I wear one on my left (forend) hand.

The vehicle should be able to take back trails, and it should be one you won't mind getting muddy, covered with dog hair, or scratched up a bit. I use an old station wagon; others I hunt with use new four-by-fours and cringe. If you have the wherewithal to have a vehicle just for hunting, you can load it up with a shooting box holding all the extras: shells; dog bells, collars, and leads; dry socks and moccasins or slippers for the ride home; an extra sweater in case things turn nasty. These can be carried in anything from an orange crate to elaborate shooting boxes made by specialty companies. Also in the car go water and a dish for the dog (the tweed hat I mentioned earlier works in a pinch), and anything else you think you might need. During the shooting season I have a sleeping bag in my car; more than once I've been too bushed for the drive home and caught a little nap after a long hunt.

Collections and Classics

The other kind of gear is the kind we tend to collect during the spell between shooting seasons, artifacts of the tradition and mystery that mold woodcock hunters into an almost primal sameness.

Let's face it: We collect prints and give to the Ruffed Grouse Society and have hat pins and shoot clay targets and have all the trappings of the sport. I think that maybe only

A fine rig for woodcock hunting: a four-wheel-drive truck with room for four shooters, and a dog trailer capable of holding four dogs. This self-contained unit also holds water and has electric lights so you can see what you are doing after dark.

trout fishermen are worse—or better—than woodcock hunters when it comes to the traditions.

Among the trappings of the sport is the collection of shooting literature, especially that dealing directly with woodcock hunting. Magazines today offer the finest literature on the topic, with the exception of some of the very old works, if you can find them in print. I think the best outdoor writers who have ever lived are alive and writing today. That's not to take anything away from William Harnden Foster *(New England Grouse Shooting)*, Colonel Harold P. Sheldon (the *Tranquillity* series), Corey Ford *(The Lower Forty)*, and on topics other than woodcock or woodcock and grouse, Havilah Babcock, Nash Buckingham, and Gordon MacQuarrie. But there are a few today who could match these legends without even breathing heavy—notably Gene Hill and George Bird Evans, especially when they write on woodcock, as they both often do.

Still, the reader of today must turn to certain magazines to get the flavor and the joys of woodcock hunting, for it is here that the real prose is found on these topics. A few of the leading ones are *Gray's Sporting Journal, Sporting Classics, Shooting Sportsman,* and *Gun Dog.* Most of the magazines share a great number of their subscribers, as The Faithful choose not one of these fine publications but several or all.

If you feel that your reading isn't reading unless it's between hard covers with no advertising, let me suggest a few titles that either are all about woodcock or feature the bird in depth. The *Tranquillity* series by Sheldon features the countryside of Vermont as a backdrop for this three-volume set, which has recently been republished for a new readership. New England in the 1920s and 1930s meant grouse and woodcock.

Anything by Corey Ford, and there were several books, is great reading. A recently rereleased version of some of his best stories is a priceless way to pass the off-season. By the way, his short story "The Road to Tinkhamtown" may be the single finest piece of sporting literature ever written. And through a line of dogs that Ford's famous Tober sired, there are Corey Ford setters hunting woodcock in the Great Lakes states each year. Those things that are fine and good do not die.

Burton Spiller's *Grouse Feathers* and *More Grouse Feathers* both feature woodcock and some striking Lynne Bogue Hunt sketches from a bygone era.

On a more contemporary note, any of Gene Hill's writings dealing with woodcock are pieces of Americana, and George Bird Evans's *The Upland Shooting Life* is already a classic.

One of the things that has recently fascinated me about woodcock shooting is the return to the tradition I mention so often. This tradition has spread to the guns, as you might expect, and there are those who would not think of shooting woodcock with anything less than a vintage Parker, an L. C. Smith, an Ithaca, or perhaps an English gun, such as a Churchill, Holland & Holland, or Purdey. These guns seem to embody the spirit of another era, especially when carried to the coverts in an old VC case or a real leg-o-mutton. I confess to being one of these traditionalists, but there is one other thing that makes tradition so especially delightful: These guns work, and they probably work better than almost anything on the market today. The collectibility of such guns makes them almost a passion in themselves, and as the double gun makes a bigger and bigger comeback on this continent, the passion is likely to become even more pervasive.

Sadly, the old doubles are a finite resource, and someday they will all be collected and they won't be passed around like they once were—or there will be too many waiting hands for each gun and some hunters are going to have to go without. If you have such a gun—and you can hit woodcock with it—keep it and don't turn it loose. There are some things more important than money.

Another Season

The season will be starting in two weeks. The gang starts showing up at my office to get in my way and keep me from finishing up so I have some time to hunt woodcock.

Charlie and Roadkill stop over and start arguing over who is the better shot, a moot point because neither of them can shoot unless they run across a star-crossed bird—that's what I tell them. They poke around through my files trying to find woodcock stories from our writers that haven't been published yet so they can read over them and salivate. They give me a bad time because they say my magazine hasn't carried enough woodcock stories lately. I throw them out finally.

They can't help it; they have the crazies, the two-weeks-before-the-season crazies. Boy, what an awful time. For weeks we've been looking for the first leaves to turn, we close our eyes and breathe deeply, trying to smell fall in the breeze at sundown. We know it's there, waiting, cold and dormant under the warmth of late summer.

My kids are out buying their school clothes, a sure sign of woodcock season in the Great Lakes. My patience is as long gone as my virtue.

The Faithful start to call in. J. D. Nelson from Nebraska calls to tell me he has two trips planned to Nova Scotia and another to Maine; Galen Winter calls from Wisconsin to tell me that the birds should trickle through this fall because the summer's been wet and that I can come anytime I want for good shooting. Anytime I want! I want right now!

I dig out my Parker and shoot some clays with it and polish it up and decide for the fourth time not to get the barrels reblued. I dig around for some No. 8s, again try to convince myself that my twenty-eight sidelock is fine for early season work and then can the idea — again. Woodcock are tradition, and my sixteen is tradition.

My dog gets walked and worked in the fields and woods near my house; the stuff is retrieved from coat pockets and wayward shooting vests and coats and arranged: shooting glasses, dog whistles, old pipes I thought I'd lost, hats, boots, shooting gloves, and all the rest.

Each shooting season brings these things, along with the feeling that here is one more opening day gone, one less day I'll have of that unknown number that's listed in The Book alongside my name, the number no one wants to know. My dog is young and in her prime, but I still wonder when her days will be up and what I'll do then because she is my friend — on many days, my best friend.

Hunting woodcock gives me, like all hunting does to most of us, a feeling of mortality; creatures live and then they die and we are, after all, creatures ourselves.

6

The Future

There was a time in the last century when woodcock shooting began on the Fourth of July. The shooting must have been phenomenal then because there are reports of a pair of shooters hunting with muzzle-loading guns taking two hundred birds in a morning.

Although those times did not last and enlightened game conservation legislation forbade further such dalliances with destruction, much of the damage had already been done, at least in the East.

In his *Tranquillity* books, written in the 1920s, Sheldon always mentions with delight any encounters with woodcock because they were so rare. But even then the numbers of birds were increasing. This increase became a flood in New England during the Great Depression and after. Farms were repossessed or just deserted as flat-broke farmers left for greener places, and the old pastures reverted to grasslands that reverted to the pioneer forests that brought the woodcock and the grouse.

It must have been something in those days to be alive and in hunting trim. We would take time away from business, you and I, to travel from New York or Boston up to Massachusetts or Maine or Vermont for the shooting. We'd load our things on a train for the daylong trip north—guns, dogs, shooting gear—and be met at the station by our New England friend. He would take us by car to an inn or perhaps his home, which we would use as our base of operations for the two weeks we'd be there.

There would be the Old Regulars to visit at the corner store and the slabs of rat cheese and pickles to munch while we tried to overcome their native standoffishness so they would tell us where the birds were this season.

But we knew our own spots in that country, and as the first frosts turned the countryside into calendar pictures, we would find the woodcock, flighting through the valleys, feeding along the alder runs, and resting away the day in the pastures now returning to forest.

But that picture has changed. Now the East is having problems with woodcock populations, and there are probably a few reasons why this is true.

A Changing Environment

First, the habitat is changing in that area of the world. The forgotten farm fields and pasture are now, fifty years later, mature forests with sterile understories and no ground cover. There is no place for the birds any more.

Because of declining woodcock populations, the bag limits have been reduced in many places in the East, and lower limits will likely continue until a solution is found to the problem.

Another reason, largely overlooked, for the decline in woodcock populations in the East could be acid rain. As most hunters know, woodcock feed primarily upon earthworms,

Author's son Chris with woodcock taken from alders that ten years earlier had been farm pasture. Such cover is one of the mainstays of woodcock shooters. Note that Chris is wet to the knees, a sure sign his old man sent him places he didn't want to go.

taking in from one to two times their own body weight each day in worms.

Now worms are mostly water, so the birds have to eat a lot of worms to keep up their strength, and even more during the stressful times when the males are skydancing and the hens are developing eggs inside their bodies or brooding the young chicks.

According to a study recorded in *The Biology and Management of the American Woodcock,* by Howard Mendall and Clarence Aldous (republished recently by Gunnerman Press; Auburn Hills, Michigan), worms in the Northeast are even more important as a food source than in other parts of the country, although I have found that the figures quoted for earthworm ingestion in New England parallel that of the Great Lakes states.

In the study the authors state: "From all available food data, it may be concluded that the woodcock feeds primarily on animal material, with earthworms and insect larvae constituting the bulk of its diet. Earthworms appear to be approximately 68% of the food over the entire range of the bird and constitute an even greater percentage of the total food in Maine and the Maritime Provinces."

Worms, then, are important to woodcock, and it stands to reason that where the worms are unavailable, the birds will not long be around. Or if the food supply is deficient during the breeding and nesting periods, fewer birds will successfully breed, nest, and hatch their young.

Worms are generally found in their greatest concentrations in soils that have a pH rating between 4.75 and 6. These ratings are weakly acidic—7 is dead neutral, and the lower the number, the higher the acid concentration.

But in the last decade or so acid rain has become a big problem. Essentially, acid rain forms when water in the atmosphere condenses into droplets in the presence of sulfur dioxide, a common byproduct of the burning of fossil fuels, especially coal. The two combine to produce sulfuric acid in a diluted state, which then falls to the earth during rain. If the temperatures are cold when the process occurs, you get acid snow.

Of the two, acid snow appears at this time to be worse because when the melt comes in the spring, the acid flow into the soil is immediate and of large volume. Huge areas in some Scandinavian countries have had forests denuded because of the effects of melting acid snow, and there and in the United States there are lakes that are virtually dead from acid rain and the runoff of acid snow.

The acid can get down to a pH of 3, which is like vinegar, and the effect of this concentrate on living things not adapted for it is deadly. Worms can survive some acidity but not the strong acid that the rains bring.

Now the woodcock head north in the spring, skydancing, courting, breeding, nesting, and brooding their eggs. Because of acid snow melt, the soil that holds the worms they need has just been inundated with acid, killing worms or retarding their populations. In other words, no worms; without worms there are no woodcock. Since the situation has existed for some time and since it has a cumulative effect on the species' population, there is every reason to believe that acid rain in the Northeast, where it is most concentrated, has had an impact on woodcock there.

This rain originates from emissions to the west and is blown to New England by the prevailing westerlies in those latitudes. But no matter where it starts, much of it ends up getting dumped on the forests of the East. Worms need the moist soils, and we know what is making those soils moist— acid rain.

Naturally, woodcock that do return and nest successfully are faced with a smaller food supply all year, so the populations will be smaller. Woodcock have few natural predators, and chick mortality is very low when compared with other ground-nesting gamebirds. So the clues to population decline have to be looked at in terms of pieces of a puzzle. I think acid rain is one clue, especially when combined with a shrinking habitat base brought about by forest maturation.

Urbanization of the Northeast and destruction of habitat in the wintering grounds are the most likely causes of the population decline.

What can be done? Obviously, strong air pollution legislation to stop or slow the causes of acid rain deposits would help. So would more habitat programs to provide woodcock with young forests in the early successional stage.

Of course, on the East Coast urban sprawl is going to allow just so much land for recreational uses. Therefore, the land that is there is going to have to be managed quite intensively for wildlife in the decades to come, and this may take some strong local legislation to stop the building of condominiums or shopping centers on bird coverts.

Migratory Mysteries

There are quite a few things about woodcock—things they share with other migratory birds—that still need explaining. For example, why do the birds so often in the late summer shuffle north from where they were born or nested only to pass right over the old home range on their way south? Maybe woodcock do it to find food in other areas during summer's dry times. But geese do it, too, according to banding studies. Are the young being genetically sent there to strengthen their flight muscles prior to migration? Nobody knows—yet.

And what is maximum carrying capacity for woodcock per acre of perfect habitat? Do we really know?

The best habitat comes about when pioneer forests emerge after fire, windstorm, or clearcutting. Clearcutting is a socially acceptable method of rejuvenating a forest. The young forests, as stated earlier, provide the critical overhead cover because they are thick, and the resulting shade tends to eliminate the troublesome grasses that woodcock find hard to move about in. Where bracken fern is present, especially in the early season, the birds have two layers of overhead cover and open ground underneath it all.

Many places look "woodcocky" because of the emerging

aspen, but they are foiled as good habitat by marsh grasses, which indicate low areas. These grasses are thick and have a tendency to mat and make walking difficult. For woodcock the moving around must be impossible—I have never moved birds in aspen with this ground cover.

In some areas of the bird's range alder is the more important species. Alder is a nitrogen-fixing plant and in effect creates its own fertility, at least for part of its lifespan. The worms come and the woodcock follow. Additionally, the alder loves the moist-to-wet soil that helps draw the worms.

In the East woodcock cover is generally habitat for woodcock only; in the western part of the bird's range ruffed grouse and woodcock are found interchangeably, often inhabiting the same coverts. This makes for some interesting shooting when the dog goes on point.

The best way to create woodcock cover seems to be to cut patches of alder or aspen or a mixture to stimulate new growth. These cut areas can be as small as an acre, but some of the better ones in the Great Lakes are large—twenty to thirty acres, like those created during timber harvests by commercial loggers or pulp cutters.

If these cuts are adjacent to or near streams with moist soils and good feeding cover, they are all the better. Birds are hunted where they rest, especially in wet years; in dry years the birds often feed and rest in the same coverts.

In the Upper Peninsula of Michigan, a drive down a dirt road just after dark will show you feeding woodcock in your headlights, many of the birds walking around right in the water, seeming to disclaim the old description of a woodcock as "a shorebird that doesn't like to get his feet wet."

The birds fly to the roads from aspen cuts on hillsides, the unintended but appreciated work of paper pulpwooders.

Cooking the 'Cock

In the old days woodcock were hunted for their meat, which was valued highly as a delicacy; today not many folks enjoy the taste. I don't shoot anything I won't eat, and I love

Author examines regenerating aspen, the best woodcock cover, especially in the Great Lakes states. Aspen regenerates after a clearcut, fire, or windstorm. For the first few years, a huge number of the plants will fight for survival, gradually thinning out and becoming well spaced. It is during their thick-growth stage that they make the best woodcock cover, providing the overhead canopy of protection the birds need.

to eat woodcock. I hang the birds—with the trail, or entrails, intact if it hasn't been shot or dog-squashed—for at least one day to allow the muscle fibers to break down. Then I skin the birds. Although many like their birds plucked rather than skinned, the truth is that woodcock are prone to carrying pesticides in the layers of fat that lie between skin and muscle tissue. Skinning allows you to discard these concentrations.

Because the bird walks little and flies a lot, the legs and thighs are white meat, whereas the breast, rich in blood vessels, is dark meat, like the rest of the migratory birds. The legs and thighs are best when they are detached, seared in a hot skillet for a minute or two, and served with a sauce as an appetizer before a game dinner.

The breasts can be treated in several ways, but here is a way that will make you love woodcock even if you've always hated woodcock.

First, hang the birds for a day in a cool breeze where insects can't get to them. Then skin out the breasts and separate them from the bone—a lot of any animal's gaminess is reduced when the meat is removed from the bone.

Next, slice the breast into strips a half-inch thick—you'll get about two slices or a little more off each side of a breast, or four per bird. Then marinate the pieces in Italian salad dressing for several hours or overnight—I don't think you can overmarinate. Get your charcoal grill fired up so that it's about as hot as you'd like it to grill a steak. Wrap each woodcock piece and a slice of Bermuda onion with one strip of bacon, securing with a toothpick. Grill these until the bacon looks edible but not crisp. The taste of woodcock, like that of all dark-meated birds, is killed by overcooking.

The resulting birds are rare, but a lot of the so-called objectionable taste is gone. These can be served as a side dish or the main course. One of my favorite game meals consists of woodcock legs and thighs as appetizers, woodcock-in-a-blanket as the first course, and ruffed grouse with wild rice as the main course. Naturally, each has to be served with its own red or white wine. Burgundy is especially good with woodcock.

As woodcock cover, this stand of aspen has "gone by." Now, natural attrition has taken place, and the surviving aspen are farther apart, and larger. Such stands offer woodcock little in the way of protection, although they may be used periodically for nesting cover. In some parts of the country there is a saying: "If you throw your hat at the ground, and it hits it, you're not in woodcock cover."

My pal Dave Wonderlich, an Easterner, likes his birds on the bone—the breasts, that is—and barely warm inside. "Blood should follow the knife" as a test for doneness, according to him. As a Midwesterner brought up with beef cooked medium, this is a habit I have little desire to acquire. Another is serving the bird with the trail right where Nature put 'em. These are supposed to be hauled out by your guests and eaten on toast. Not me, brother, at least not in the immediate future or in any state of sobriety.

One way to collect enough good woodcock for a meal is by watching your shooting. Early in the season the birds flush so close and shots are so quick that a ruined bird is often the case. I remember one bird I centered with my Parker when I first got it. The bird disappeared at eight feet, and only two wings were left. I was sick over the waste. So if you get the chance, say with an easy straightaway through relatively open cover, try fringing the bird with the side of the pattern. With fine shot (No. 8 or No. 9), this isn't as hard as it sounds. If you have the time, let the bird get out a bit and hold right on him for the same result.

My older son, Chris, has started passing up easy shots at woodcock—rising birds caught in open cover over a point. Or he will try fringing them for the table. By the way, if you announce that you plan to do this before the hunt starts, your excuse machine is oiled and humming smoothly for when—not if—you miss.

Future Habitats, Future Hunters

I think that the future of woodcock in this country will be tied to land-use practices, which include forest management for the bird. Luckily, except to the most narrow viewpoints, managing woodcock can be carried on as a side benefit to managing whitetail deer and ruffed grouse, along with cutting timber for pulpwood. As soon as some eastern states realize that vegetation eighty feet in the air does nothing for woodcock—and grouse and deer—there will be some changes made and we'll see populations rise, my expressed fears about acid rain notwithstanding.

Efforts for the Future

A workshop on the role of woodcock habitat management in commercial timber harvesting activities was held in Portland, Maine, on September 10, 1987. The meeting was attended by more than eighty corporate and public foresters, wildlife biologists, and other interested individuals. Participating in this workshop were the American Forest Council, the Ruffed Grouse Society, the Wildlife Management Institute, and the U.S. Fish and Wildlife Service. I am grateful to Brad Bortner of the U.S. Fish and Wildlife Service's office of migratory bird management in Laurel, Maryland, for providing me with the recommendations that came out of this workshop. I am going to quote directly from the draft summary of the workshop's activities.

On technical assistance. "There was strong agreement on the need for creation of teams of biologists and foresters within each state to provide technical assistance to industrial foresters. These teams would assist in refining timber management plans for the benefit of wildlife while also maintaining timber production. Team biologists would also be available to make management suggestions during 'on-the-ground assistance' tours. Teams would be made up of state and industry biologists with consultation with federal representatives when appropriate. Assignment to teams could be accomplished through professional exchanges and would foster further communication between members and their organizations. Demonstration areas could be established to provide examples of actual recommendations of a team. Company biologists would also receive training in wildlife habitat analysis and management."

On information and education. "Additional information and education programs were also recommended. This would include sponsoring additional workshops on the application of silvicultural prescriptions and other habitat management techniques, establishment of regional demonstration areas, and production of popular articles and 'how to' videos."

On landowner incentives. "Wildlife habitat management can be costly and decrease corporate profits, so financing issues were discussed. Hunting leases and permit fees are common on industrial land in the South while uncommon in northern states. Participants suggested that companies further explore this practice to determine if fee access programs would be practical for implementation on their lands. It was recommended that a catalog of existing state incentive programs for landowners be prepared. From this catalog it would be possible to investigate the need for additional programs to assist landowners. A landowner recognition program, similar to the American Tree Farm System, was also proposed. Programs of this type are effective in promoting wildlife management on a local basis because neighbors become interested in participating after observing the success of an adjacent landowner."

On coordination and communication. "Agency coordination and improved communication was identified as needing improvement. It was suggested that the Forest Service and the Fish and Wildlife Service establish a coordinated network for technical information transfer to professionals and establish demonstration areas on federal lands (i.e., national forests and national wildlife refuges). Improved lines of communication are also needed within flyways and regions and should include woodcock biologists from southern states. It was recommended that workshops on habitat problems be held with wildlife biologists and foresters from southeastern states. The need to cooperate and establish joint ventures with the Cooperative Extension Service and Soil Conservation Service was also discussed."

On research and management programs. "While not directly associated with woodcock habitat management in the Northeast, several other topics were mentioned. These included the need for more research on woodcock habitat requirements and survival rates in woodcock wintering areas, and for an improved sampling framework to survey woodcock hunters that would provide unbiased estimates of harvests. The necessity of research on wintering woodcock was stressed by several groups who had firsthand knowledge of habitat losses and increased mortality rates among woodcock in southern states. Participants suggested initiation of new studies to investigate these problems and a general increase in research commitment. It has been known for at least ten years that improvement is needed in harvest data collection. The present wing collection survey, annually conducted by the Fish and Wildlife Service, is a nonrandom sample of experienced woodcock hunters and duck hunters who also hunt woodcock. In order to improve reliability of the harvest survey, participants recommended that a national woodcock hunting permit be established. This permit would allow managers to sample woodcock hunters randomly to determine hunting activity and success, harvest, and other data on harvest distribution and composition."

On outlook for the future. "The workshop was generally acknowledged as a successful first step in improving cooperation for better woodcock management. We strongly urge acceptance of the group's recommendations and continued efforts to manage woodcock cooperatively. Formation of state–industry teams should be accomplished during 1988. We believe the formation of a standing committee to guide the implementation of the workshop's recommendations would greatly improve the outlook on the future of woodcock. We urge the organization of a similar workshop for foresters and wildlife biologists in southern states within the next year and one in the central region (Midwest) in the following year."

It is obvious a number of people are concerned about woodcock. Fortunately, many of these people are also in positions to do something about declining woodcock populations. It is also obvious that most of the experts who regularly study and manage woodcock in exchange for paychecks believe that the key to higher woodcock populations is proper habitat manipulation of the young pioneer forest. Woodcock hunters all along the bird's range certainly hope their efforts meet with success.

I also think the future is tied to those who hunt and shoot. America is changing, and for the better. Today's shooters are starting to realize that the days when a hunt's success was measured by a full game bag are gone. Part of this change in attitude is because the hordes of game are not as they once were, but it also has to do with the maturation process of the hunting population.

Once we mature as shooters and as sportsmen to those final stages in which the experience is the important, measurable aspect of any hunt, we come to appreciate woodcock more. Woodcock seem to draw this appreciation out of hunters more rapidly than many other birds do, and we come to view each bird encountered—shot or missed—as a unique, savored experience.

Just as the British a century or more ago chose a code of ethics and sporting behavior, so are we choosing. It had to come, it was a matter of time, and it is probably involved somehow with the realization that the wilderness is indeed finally beaten back. That's why we see the double guns and expensive pointing dogs and tweed hats and thornproof coats on rainy days. The bird brings out the good things in us.

Gone Hunting

Dawn hasn't quite won its battle with night when I nudge my station wagon down the trail that once was a logging road. The headlights bounce as I hit ruts for a quarter mile until I come to my turnoff. It isn't really a turnoff, just a wide spot in the trail where I can get the car off in case some Neanderthal in a jacked-up Chevy truck comes barreling through looking for mudholes he can thrash around in.

The sky is bright enough that I can start seeing the outlines of the trees off to the right, low alders and fifteen-foot aspens mixing and marrying with each other, tolerating each other. If the birds are there, they have returned not long ago from feeding down by the little brook. I roll down the window so I can hear it, the sound brooks make, the freedom sound of rushing water. There, I know, the dark, fragile-looking trout are finning out their redds in the shortening days of October.

I can't stand it any more, so I get out of the car and open the tailgate and sit on it, smoking my pipe and trying to keep from letting Jess know I am as excited as she is. She is summer fat but she is ready, her pink tongue lolling, and she reaches out to kiss me, sticking her tongue in my ear. From December to September each year she runs the house, demanding that you share anything you're eating, even from the table. She sleeps on beds and furniture, and she won't move for company. She's haughty, spreading her fat setter body and her orange-and-white setter hair all over everything. She won't mind me worth a damn-and-a-half for ten months of the year, but in October she smooches me on the ear and begs me to take her woodcock hunting. In October she is my love slave.

The sun is higher, at least the promise of the sun is higher, so I start the ritual. On come the boots—knee-high rubber boots, for it has been a wet fall and a wetter summer. Next the whistle with the little, tortuous toot for Jess, who answers with a whine almost above human hearing. Then my hat and vest and shooting gloves because the vines and briars will tear at me all day. Finally, the old Parker. I dump in a box of No. 8s, more an act of faith than anything else, for this is a small covert and I wouldn't shoot twenty-five times even if I had the chance. Now we are ready.

Dawn has come, as it comes in my part of the world in autumn, all at once. The blue sky holds a sun that sets fire to the aspens. Among them a wayward red maple burns without heat like Moses' bush.

We walk the path and I send Jess ahead and in. Her bell falls silent, and I give a little whistle, my way of asking her if she's serious, or watching a squirrel, or taking a leak. She doesn't give me an answering ring, so I walk in. She is staunch like the old pro that she is, but the puppy that still lives within her quivers. I carry my sixteen high and ready; the woodcock, a young male, twitters up, barely beating my heart up to my neck level. As he starts away, I swing the double on him.

Just before I press the front trigger, I smile. "Hello, little friend."

Other Books by Steve Smith

Hunting Ducks and Geese

Hunting Upland Gamebirds

Picking Your Shots

Outdoor Yarns and Outright Lies, by Gene Hill and Steve Smith

ZN-95